Architectural Excellence
in a Diverse World Culture

William T. Baker

Philae Temple, Aswan, Egypt

Architectural Excellence in a Diverse World Culture

William T. Baker

Introduction by Michael J. Crosbie

images
Publishing

Dedicated to the Architects and Designers of the new Millennium

Published in Australia in 2008 by
The Images Publishing Group Pty Ltd
ABN 89 059 734 431
6 Bastow Place, Mulgrave, Victoria 3170, Australia
Tel: +61 3 9561 5544 Fax: +61 3 9561 4860
books@imagespublishing.com
www.imagespublishing.com

Copyright © The Images Publishing Group Pty Ltd 2008
The Images Publishing Group Reference Number: 771

All rights reserved. Apart from any fair dealing for the purposes of private study, research, criticism or review as permitted under the Copyright Act, no part of this publication may be reproduced, stored in a retrieval system or transmitted in any form by any means, electronic, mechanical, photocopying, recording or otherwise, without the written permission of the publisher.

National Library of Australia Cataloguing-in-Publication entry:

Author:	Baker, William T.
Title:	Architectural excellence : in a diverse world culture / author, William T. Baker.
Publisher:	Mulgrave, Vic. : Images, 2008.
ISBN:	978 1 86470 279 8 (hbk.)
Notes:	Includes index. Bibliography.
Subjects:	Architecture, Classical. Architecture, Modern. Architecture—Aesthetics. Architecture—Indian influences. Architecture—Middle Eastern influences. Architecture—Oriental influences. Architecture—Western influences.

Dewey Number: 720.92

Edited by Beth Browne

Designed by Kent Hatterick and Amanda Byrom, Beck Premedia Workflow Compression

Production by The Graphic Image Studio Pty Ltd, Mulgrave, Australia
www.tgis.com.au

Pre-publishing services by Splitting Image Colour Studio Pty Ltd, Australia

Printed by Everbest Printing Co. Ltd., in Hong Kong/China

IMAGES has included on its website a page for special notices in relation to this and our other publications. Please visit www.imagespublishing.com.

PAGE ONE: CARVED STONE RELIEF PANEL OF AN ISLAMIC DESIGN.   PRECEDING PAGES: VILLAGE OF OIA, SANTORINI, GREECE.

CONTENTS

PREFACE — x

INTRODUCTION — xiv

CHAPTER 1: ARCHITECTURE IS THE PRIMARY ART — 1
Diversity and Variety—The Role of Architecture in a Culture—The Role of Ornament—The Role of Building Forms

CHAPTER 2: THE CLASSICAL IDEAL — 14
Classicism Defined—The Role of Good Taste—The Role of Genius

CHAPTER 3: TRADITION AS THE BASIS FOR EXCELLENCE — 22
Novelty and the Bizarre—Tradition in Greek Architecture—Tradition in Roman Architecture—Tradition in Chinese Architecture—Tradition in the Architecture of the European Renaissance—Tradition in French Neo-Classicism—Tradition in Swedish Neo-Classicism—Tradition in the English Arts and Crafts Movement

CHAPTER 4: RATIONALISM AS THE BASIS FOR EXCELLENCE — 50
Ancient Sources—Proportional Guidelines—Rationalism in Other Cultures

CHAPTER 5: NATURE AS THE BASIS FOR EXCELLENCE — 66
Scale—Proportion—Rhythm—Symmetry—Scientific Studies of Nature

CHAPTER 6: FUNCTION AS THE BASIS FOR EXCELLENCE — 76
The Amphitheater—Basilicas and Cathedrals—Houses—Tall Buildings

CHAPTER 7: MATERIALS AND EXCELLENCE — 90
Noble Materials—Base Materials—Modern Materials—Architecture as Sculpture

CHAPTER 8: TIME IS THE FINAL ARBITER — 102
Casa Mila—New York Library—Stadhuset, Stockholm—Villa Savoie—Chapel at Ronchamp—Rockefeller Center—Crow Island School—Farnsworth House—Lever House—Seagram Building—Venturi House—One Atlantic Center—National Gallery of Art—Pompidou Centre

CHAPTER 9: THE NEW MILLENNIUM — 116
The Challenge as Voiced by Others—The Challenge of Expediency—The Challenge of Educational Training—The Challenge of Government Patronage—A Call for Excellence in Design

ACKNOWLEDGEMENTS — 120

NOTES — 122

INDEX — 129

FOLLOWING PAGES: TEMPLE OF PURA ULUN, DANU BRATAN, BALI.

Lama Temple, Beijing, China.

PREFACE

We live in an age where the aesthetic principles of the past are deemed to have lost their relevance and authority. It is timely, therefore, to review those principles to discover in what ways they can speak anew to our time. As a building designer with a keen appreciation for tradition-based architecture, I believe a study of the principles underlying the aesthetics of architectural design is more relevant than ever before. Ours is an age of short-lived architecture generally lacking a sense of permanence. It is an age that is not building for the future, perhaps because the future appears so bleak. It is an age in which speculative development is driving architectural design more than any great movement from within the architectural profession itself. Contributing to this situation are the industry professionals, the gatekeepers so to speak, who have systematically rejected the idea that such principles are relevant to architectural design. They have adopted a design philosophy that places a premium on creativity but with no real unifying theory to guide that creativity. The loss of objective criteria by which architecture may be properly judged diminishes all architecture as a result. My desire is to present these principles to practitioners and students of architecture to establish a common basis for critical analysis.

Of equal concern to me is the ongoing trend among the world's societies of adopting a culturally void architecture. Societies do this to the detriment of their own culture and the impoverishment of world culture as a collective whole. It is disturbing to visit foreign lands and find that the general architecture of new buildings strongly resembles the character of one's own. Variety and diversity, not uniformity, should be the goal.

Professionals and scholars of our time have not addressed this growing dilemma of architectural uniformity. In fact, they appear to be endorsing it by their silence. There is a need for a statement of theory that is relevant for today that speaks to the contemporary needs of divergent cultures. A new sense of inspiration and direction is needed within the professional community for the design of retail, commercial, religious, and governmental structures. These are the buildings that form the core fabric of our societies and impact the daily lives of our citizens.

While these principles may seem self-evident to some or irrelevant to others, it is important that they be acknowledged and taught as part of the standard academic curriculum. There can be no success in architecture or in city building without some coherent underlying unity of thought about the design process. It is relevant to this discussion to ask, why is it that some buildings endear themselves to a society more than others? Likewise, why is it that such buildings are more often old than new? The answer to these questions can be found in five principles.

I also wish to address the two subjects most frequently ignored by contemporary architectural critics and academics—tradition and ornament. Their relevance has been marginalized yet their absence in our architecture impoverishes our cities and our world culture. Tradition and ornament need not be seen as a threat to be avoided. Rather, they are a continuation of a culture's heart and soul. These are the elements that distinguish one people from another. Architecture without these two foundational members becomes anti-cultural, void of collective memory, and transient in nature. The traditions of a culture have an important role in any architecture that seeks to speak to its time and place. Likewise, ornament is the voice of architecture that speaks of the natural creative expression of a people. By stripping architecture of ornament, our buildings are robbed of that which enriches visually and culturally. Only when modern practice is reconciled with these two elements of design will we be able to continue our long journey of creating a living architecture of excellence for all peoples.

This work encompasses two major themes. The first examines the five principles underlying the aesthetics of architectural design and reviews examples from around the world illustrating these principles. Through this discussion, it will be seen that the principles of design are culturally neutral and more pervasive than any single culture from our collective past. The principles that lead to excellence in architecture are just as relevant to the buildings of Asia as they are to the buildings of the West. Furthermore, no one culture can claim architectural perfection as its own. This is a conceit whose time has come to an end. The principles of aesthetics presented herein are found in the architecture of all the nations and peoples of the world. All can achieve its perfection and many do.

The second theme is the challenge posed by the premise that such principles do in fact exist. A survey of built work illustrating these principles, as well as those buildings that do not, is presented for further discussion. Through these examples, it will be apparent that fashion has always affected architecture as it does any art form. However, fashion is not a threat to architectural excellence. When guided by the five principles, fashion can lead architecture to new heights.

The principles outlined in this book are meant to promote discussion and further study among the professional community. Rather than provide a dogmatic approach to design, my purpose is to embolden each culture to develop its own unique voice in its architectural expression in a dynamic way. The important issue of architectural aesthetics deserves to be considered in an unbiased way by academics and professionals alike. To anyone concerned with architectural aesthetics, these principles offer a guide to achieve the tripartite goal of strength, usefulness, and beauty as first voiced by Vitruvius 2,000 years ago. The act of building well is of paramount concern to every society because of the lasting legacy it creates for generations to come.

William T. Baker
Atlanta, Georgia

Harem, Amber Fort, Jaipur, India.

INTRODUCTION
BACK TO THE CENTER

Virtual realities, global communities, building information management, sustainability, real-time design, high performance, synthetic environments, critical path, fast-track construction, design/build. This is the world of architecture today: immediate, simultaneous, fleeting, edgy.

In such a world, it is easy to forget why one became an architect, to lose sight of what kindled within each one of us a heated passion for the art of building. William Baker's book brings you back to the center. He beckons you to return to the temple, to run your fingers over the touchstone of your calling, and remind yourself why you are an architect. He shows the traditions of our craft, the perennial beauties of architecture, the awe-filled history of our creations. Across time, across space, and across culture, Baker lays out the objects of our desire, the artifacts to which each one of us aspires as an architect.

It is easy to be distracted. The business of architecture, the demands of schedules, the never-ending struggles with project team members—all of it pulls us away from the center, throws us against the wall of expediency, pushes us toward half-hearted solutions. "Good enough," you relent. "A hundred years from now, what difference will it make?" Baker reminds us about the difference. This is why you became an architect, he counsels, this is why you pour out your heart for your art.

This book will annoy some people. A superficial reading might lead one to dismiss it as being too traditional, too conservative, and irrelevant to the world we live in. Architects are innovators, after all. Where is the futuristic vision? How do we make architecture so that it touches people around the globe, makes a difference in their lives, solves their problems today? However, read more deeply, this book challenges us to look at architecture's traditions not as ready-made answers, but as departure points for fashioning responses that are appropriate in terms of scale, function, durability, place, history, and reproducibility. Baker correctly identifies this last quality as the key one in our role as responsible professionals. Architecture that is socially relevant and responsible is always reproducible.

Other readers will get hung up on the illustrations of column capitals and architraves: dead white guy architecture. But look closer. Baker draws his examples from east and west, north and south. The pleasures of architecture, and what they teach us, are found around the world. The lessons of architecture are truly global in their relevance and in their pedigree. This truly is architecture's International Style, and by style I don't mean a collection of easily codified mannerisms. The International Style that Baker writes about with passion in this book comes in many different accents, flavors, and inflections. But it shares traits across continents.

Scale and proportion are found in traditional architecture around the globe. While the details of regional and national styles change, sensitive scale is timeless. We perceive it when we look at the Parthenon in Athens, the Pantheon in Rome, Hagia Sophia in Istanbul. Windows, doors, columns, wall panels, and moldings work in unison to relate a building to our body so that we can immediately understand its relation in size to our own. Often these elements have anthropomorphic qualities (the column capital is the head, the shaft is the torso, the base is the feet). Scale makes architecture intelligible on a basic human level, and buildings with carefully calibrated scale are found around the world, from all different periods.

Related to scale is ornament—another element that has universal appeal. Inside and out, ornament is a delight to the eye. Ornament is often inspired by the region, based on local flora, colors, and patterns. It aids in our appraisal of how big the building is and how and where we might penetrate it. It can regulate architecture's composition, lending its pieces a sense of hierarchy. Frequently bearing evidence of handcraft, ornament can provide a humanistic connection to architecture. Ornament can relay history—the earliest methods of building construction, for example, or how the architecture was shaped by environmental factors. Ornament is part of architecture's narrative: it helps buildings tell their stories.

The materials of architecture provide us with information about the building's status in the society. Baker writes about "noble" and "base" materials: the former being more durable and reserved for culturally significant buildings, the latter used for less important and less costly structures. In a world where any material can be used anywhere in the world, you might think that these distinctions are no longer important. But they remain valid and critical for a number of reasons. First, wherever you design, there are regional versions of "noble" and "base" materials, so your choice helps to root the building in its location. Also, we know that regional materials are better choices for reasons of sustainability. The choice of materials can make architecture intelligible to anyone, thus establishing a dialogue between people and buildings. Ultimately, material choice can militate against the sense of "placelessness" that pervades our contemporary built world. It not only roots a building to a place, it helps us to form ideas of who we are and the place in which we live. It gives us identity.

The commonality of all the features described above is their essential "humanness." Scale, ornament, color, pattern, order, and materials are all features that we readily relate to as human beings. These are not elements that need to be "translated" for non-architects—most anyone can understand them, relate to them, and feel at home with them. This is what makes the architecture that Baker celebrates universal and timeless: the buildings to which we are drawn across epochs speak to us about what makes us human.

Toward the end of this book, Baker reminds us that architecture of excellence is always in harmony with Nature. It is in harmony with the nature of building traditions that we share over cultures and over centuries. It is in harmony with the nature of how our structures serve the needs of our daily lives and the extraordinary demands of our spiritual lives. Ultimately, it is in harmony with the nature of a life in architecture, clearing away all of the detritus of contemporary practice and discovering anew why you are an architect.

Michael J. Crosbie

An architect, writer, critic, and teacher, Dr. Crosbie is the Chairman of the Department of Architecture at the University of Hartford.

HAGIA SOPHIA, ISTANBUL, TURKEY.

Figure 1. Papyrus Columns. Temple at Karnak. Thebes. Egypt.

CHAPTER 1
ARCHITECTURE IS THE PRIMARY ART

Architecture is no less than the primary art of a nation and is one of the noblest acts of human activity.[1] It provides shelter, one of the first and fundamental needs of humankind. It provides the setting for the display of a culture's public life. It encloses the space in which people worship their gods. It is the mother of all arts because it provides a canvas upon which the artistic trades apply their craft. It supports the numerous trades and professions that are critical to a nation's development. Furthermore, the very act of creating architecture and the ability to appreciate the beauty of it appears to be uniquely human. This fact suggests that we should seek to better understand the origins of this innate creativity and the role beauty plays in fulfilling a deep-seated need in human nature.[2]

Those who practice the art of architecture and the craft of building are the custodians of the physical fabric of our nations, our cities, and our neighborhoods. The architect is foremost because it is he or she who takes the intangible hopes and dreams of a people and translates them into a working drawing for construction. The builder completes the task by creating the tangible structure expressing the architect's vision in stone, wood, glass, and steel. It is no easy task, and therefore, governments, universities, and businesses should take the lead to encourage high standards for design and building construction. In this way, our architecture will more ably weather the test of time. By making such a commitment, each culture's built environment will stand as a lasting testimony of its aspirations for the future.

The guiding principles that produce great architecture are culturally neutral. These principles are not biased toward one cultural norm over another. They do not have in their origin any tie to a particular ancient culture, nor do they pretend to make a value judgment on one society's superiority over another. They are universal in their truth and application. When followed in their intent and spirit, they produce an architecture that is unique to that society, is indigenous in its spirit, and ennobles a people by creating a strong sense of community and place. The principles are:

- *Great architecture provides continuity with the traditions of a shared past.*
- *Great architecture has rationalism as its basis.*
- *Great architecture follows Nature's scale, proportion, rhythm, and symmetry.*
- *Great architecture bases its form on its function.*
- *Great architecture is wise in its choice of materials.*

Architecture developed according to these principles is better positioned to prove itself enduring over time and come to be considered architecture of excellence. This is the ultimate goal for any architectural style—to mature; to stand the test of time; to be perfected as it is repeated by multiple generations. When architecture achieves this lofty goal, then it speaks with a voice that transcends its originating culture and can be admired and appreciated by people from other world cultures. When certain buildings achieve this distinction—and there have been many—the world takes notice and architecture is changed, never to be the same again. While many societies have achieved this goal in their built work, it is possible for every culture to do so regardless of its size, wealth, or natural resources. All societies can create their own architecture of excellence. And through deliberate and thoughtful effort, each should be encouraged to do so.

Diversity and Variety
If we observe Nature, and the many facets of its design, we find that the natural order of creation is one of fantastic variety and diversity. Whether plant, animal, or the elements, diversity is the common denominator. In color, texture, and

form, all of these contain an infinite variety that is incomprehensible. Should not the works of our hands emulate Nature by creating an architecture that demonstrates this same creativity?

Our best buildings are enriched through diversity and variety of ornament, sculpture, painting, and the art of the metalworker's craft. In the great buildings of past civilizations, these related arts are incorporated in important and prominent ways to enrich the overall fabric of the building. Sculpture in particular is used to create an interesting play of light and shadow across the façade. These sculptural elements were often purely decorative, sometimes highly symbolic, never boring. It is the architect who is responsible for thoughtfully incorporating these works into the fabric of the building. It is he or she who is responsible for orchestrating the composition to achieve a complementary whole. When the architect is a person of talent, these buildings are a reflection of their time and place. When the architect is a person of genius, these buildings transcend his or her time and place and become cultural icons that are universally admired for generations.

Because diversity and variety is the rule and not the exception, the challenge for each society and culture is to produce architecture that is a true reflection of itself, contributing to the diversity of the world's built environment. The necessary component to achieve this goal is the development of an architectural vocabulary that is true to its people, their hopes, dreams, and aspirations. When one culture successfully accomplishes this task, it is often the case that other cultures adopt this successful architectural vocabulary without developing one of their own. To avoid this error, each culture must have the confidence and discipline to look squarely at itself to determine what is true and good about itself and what it wishes to say about its past and its hopes for the future through its architecture.

The Role of Architecture in a Culture
The power of architecture can be harnessed to help a culture achieve its mission to develop a noble society. The built environment's effect on a society's culture and its belief about itself is often ignored but is important to understand. Architecture has a pivotal role in how a society views itself and its place in the world. A society's buildings should express a hope and commitment to the future. This requires economic commitment and an interest in the greater good of the built environment for the community at large. Building only for the short run, and as cheaply as possible, seldom results in a noble built environment. Such construction is a poor use of the world's natural resources because buildings of this sort often reach the end of their life expectancy within a decade or so of their construction. These buildings represent a worst-case scenario because their demise cries out to their lack of true aesthetic value, the impermanence of materials used, or their failure as a plan to provide usefulness over a long period of time. In contrast, architecture of excellence is characterized by buildings that stand the test of time; by buildings of long use with layers of history that add richness to a culture; and by a built environment that inspires and delights its citizens. This is not a utopian vision. There have been numerous societies in our common past that deliberately pursued these inspiring goals and succeeded. Should we do any less?

Figure 2. Reconstruction of the Ishtar Gate.

Figure 3. Great Pyramid, Chichen Itza, Yucatan.

Architecture also serves as a built memorial for those who created it. Entire civilizations are remembered primarily because of the architectural record that has come down to us. Egypt is one example of a civilization that succeeded in creating buildings and monuments that embody the memory and grandeur that was once theirs. They sought immortality through the construction of pyramids and massive temple complexes with distinctive obelisks, pylons, and lotus and papyrus columns (figure 1). The Egyptians' buildings had a useful life span of thousands of years. Their buildings were unique statements representing their culture and remain successful icons today despite the fact that the civilization that produced them is long gone. Another culture remembered primarily because of its architectural record is that of Mesopotamia (figure 2). Most of what we know about ancient Mesopotamian culture is due to the architectural fabric that has been preserved despite millennia of man-made destruction and erosion. Greece and Rome created great public architecture of beauty and grace, the remains of which still enchant visitors 2,000 years later. Even in some of the more remote parts of the world, civilizations that had vanished before Western discovery, such as the Mayans of the Yucatan, are remembered solely because of their architectural record in stone. Their step pyramids, beautifully carved stonework, and ornamental reliefs are silent witnesses to the glory of a people who were one of the dominant civilizations of Central America (figure 3).

The Role of Ornament

To abandon ornament in architecture is to divorce architecture from its culture. While there are those who advocate stripping our buildings down to their most basic geometry, devoid of ornamentation, it is the buildings that embrace the artistic trades and revel in variety and diversity of ornament that are the greatest pleasure to our senses. In the 20th century, architectural theorists such as Adolf Loos (1870–1933) saw ornament as something negative to be removed. His 1908 essay declared, "The evolution of culture marches with the elimination of ornament from articles of everyday use."[3] In the same year, the Dutch architect Berlage (1856–1934) voiced the same opinion when he wrote, "And thus in architecture, decoration and ornament are quite inessential while space-creation and the relationships of masses are its true essentials."[4] Others, such as Ralph Weber, rejected ornament on the grounds of its passing relevance for a modern culture. He said, "The strategy of using history as a quarry of forms can only produce socio-romantic drapery because the forms thus discovered originated in socio-cultural conditions and life patterns we no longer share."[5] These men objected to the use of ornamental details out of a mistaken belief that such details can no longer speak to the needs of contemporary culture. While meanings may change over time, ornament can still perform its primary task of delighting the eye. Now that time has passed, we can reassess this rejection of ornament with the advantage of hindsight from a large body of work embracing the "less is more" approach to architecture.

The removal of ornament from architecture occurred at the same time that a number of innovative building materials were being introduced—glass curtain walls among them. Chicago architect Bertrand Goldberg (1913–1997), a proponent of the Bauhaus and Modernist schools, experimented with glass curtain walled buildings devoid of ornament and offered a first-hand opinion on this subject. After years of experimentation with steel and glass, he expresses his frustration that, "The glass creates a certain aesthetic expression that is undaring, limited, even boring, and in many ways a denial of those things that have some kind of human significance: light, shade, and texture. Although the glass wall has a texture of its own, it is not one that readily communicates with the world around it."[7] Thus, he testifies to the aesthetic limitations of glass as a primary cladding material.

In contrast to the typical unornamented glass box, our buildings should make use of ornamentation that speaks to the culture in which it is built. In some societies, a well-established ornamental vocabulary already exists and has been in place for centuries. Other societies have yet to develop an ornamental vocabulary that represents them as a people. Once developed, a society's architecture is better able to take its unique place in the world. To do so, it must have confidence in itself and seek to find that which is expressive of its very being. Each society has the ability to create its own architectural vocabulary and should not be intimidated by the task. The architect's role in this matter is that of a leader. It is he or she who must serve as an advocate for the best artistic talent and material resources available.

As explained by the Renaissance architect Alberti, "for some (ornaments) please us by

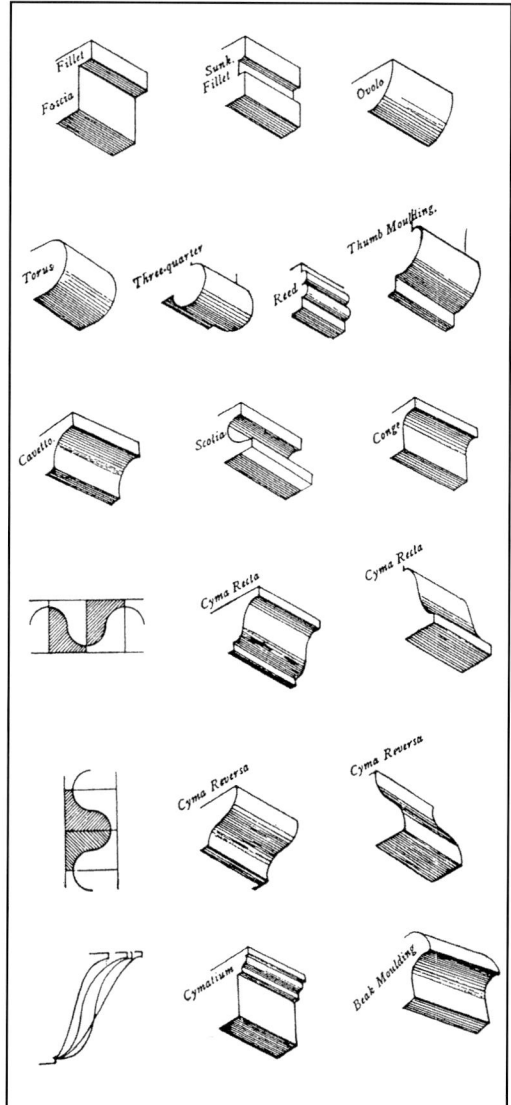

FIGURE 4. MOLDING PROFILES. WILLIAM R. WARE, *AMERICAN VIGNOLA* (NORTON LIBRARY, 1977). P. 7.

their largeness, others with being little, and others moderate. One part therefore should be terminated with straight lines, another with curve, and another again with straight and curve mixed together; provided you observe the caution I have so often given you, to avoid falling into the error of excess, so as to seem to have made a monster with limbs disproportionate."[6]

Ornament is often characterized by its variety of molding profiles. Architects over the millennia have considered the design of moldings to be an expressive part of the art of architecture and, as such, designed them with careful attention to proportion and form. As observed by Viollet-le-Duc, "All the moldings of the beautiful Greek architecture had been caressed, shall I say, with studious love."[8] The four basic categories of profiles are: plane, convex, concave, and double curvature. These can be found throughout the world's architecture. Variations on these basic profiles have resulted in at least 16 distinct profiles (figure 4). Moldings grace our buildings by providing light and shadow contrasts. Furthermore, they can establish a foundation, mark a height, define an opening, support a projection, or conceal a joint. They are named in the first position, a base or plinth; in the second, a stringcourse; in the third, a frame or casing; and in the fourth, an entablature (figure 5). While it is possible to create architecture devoid of ornament, this in no way precludes the value of ornament as a valid component of architecture. Rather than rejecting it, ornament should be embraced and developed. It is ornament that provides a delight to the eye by breaking up a façade with its play of shadow and light. It is ornament that provides a never ceasing visual delight with some new element to observe each time a building is experienced. This layering of visual interest is true to Nature itself. If one looks at anything found in Nature, one discovers that there is always another detail or something new to see upon closer examination.

The Louvre, Paris, France

One of the great buildings of the world that uses ornament to capture the spirit and aspirations of a nation is the Louvre in Paris. Although it was originally designed as a fortress in 1190, it has been transformed over time into one of the great palace complexes of Europe. One of the most significant additions to the Louvre occurred in 1549 when Henri II commissioned the architect Lescot to design a new wing containing a grand reception hall. The new architecture of

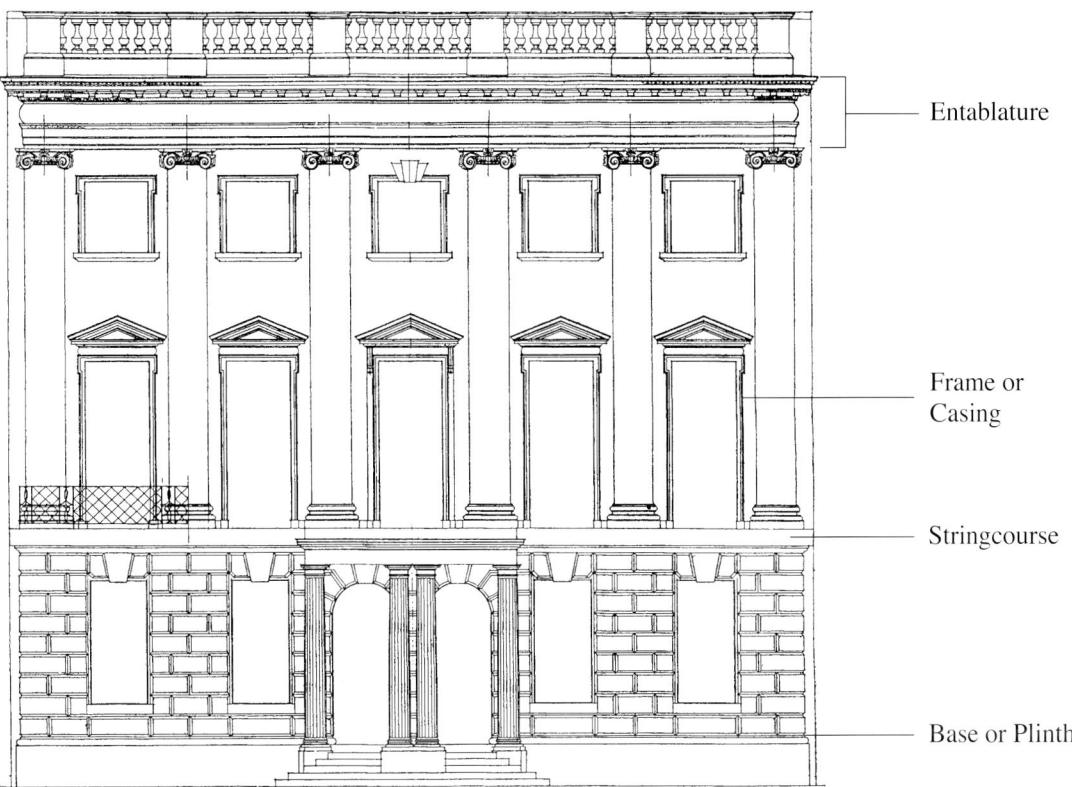

Figure 5. Architectural features on a building. Colin Amery, *Period Houses and their Details* (Architectural Press, 1974), Plate 2.

the Louvre was intended to symbolize in stone France's desire to proclaim itself heir to all that was great from ancient Greek culture. The Lescot wing demonstrates a mastery of classical motifs and a new interpretation of those forms within the context of French culture.

The Lescot wing was an advanced building form of its time that makes many references to a much older tradition. Lescot shows great talent in his use of Greek ornament to communicate the king's desire to associate his reign with the glories of ancient Greece. This is especially evident in the Salle des Caryatides, so named because of its sculptural group that is inspired by the Porch of the Caryatides found on the Athenian Acropolis (figure 6). These supporting columns in the form of maidens are so named, according to Vitruvius, because they represent the maidens from Caryae in Laconia who were led away as captives by the conquering Greeks. To memorialize their perpetual slavery, their images were transformed into architectural supports portraying them carrying the structural load of the roof. These caryatides are described in the first French edition of Vitruvius (1547) translated by Jean Martin and partially illustrated by the sculptor Jean Goujon. Goujon's illustrations are superior to those of earlier editions and show an exceptional interpretation of these Greek caryatides. Three years later, Goujon was given the chance to execute caryatides of his own design for Lescot's new gallery at the Louvre.

Goujon's porch is located at one end of the main reception hall, not on the outside of the building as is the prototype in Greece. Furthermore, it is designed for an entirely different purpose. Rather than serving as a protective covering, as does the original at the Acropolis, this porch serves as an interior platform for the court musicians. The porch's four sculptural columns (figure 7), created by Goujon, are no doubt inspired by his own illustrations of three years earlier. Rather than being a mere copy of the originals, however, Goujon creates his own version of the type.

Figure 6. Porch of the Caryatides, Acropolis, Athens, Greece.

Figure 7. Porch of the Caryatides, The Louvre, Paris, France.

Furthermore, Lescot continues his reference to the ornaments found on the Acropolis in his use of ornamental egg-and-dart moldings, dentils, and Greek key motifs. He also adds additional sculptural ornament modeled after Roman prototypes incorporating them throughout the hall and on its limestone exterior (figure 8).

This building is significant because Lescot successfully references a previous culture's architecture while his new structure is something entirely different from any building found in ancient Greece. Even more striking is the fact that Lescot's building, which makes extensive use of Greek ornamental details, succeeds in creating a unique architectural statement that appears authentically French rather than Greek. Evidence of Lescot's success lies in the fact that his building set a precedent for future additions to the palace by later monarchs. Today, the Louvre serves as a powerful expression of French culture and is a proclamation in stone of France's continuity with the traditions of Western civilization.

Following pages: Figure 8. Lescot Wing, The Louvre, Paris, France.

FIGURE 9. THE TAJ MAHAL, AGRA, INDIA.

The Role of Building Forms

In addition to its ornamental vocabulary, each culture must guard against losing those architectural forms and details that are specific to its national identity. These include shapes and forms such as uniquely shaped domes, distinctive arches, elegantly flared roofs, or characteristic gabled roofs (figure 10). In each case, these forms were developed independently and are indigenous to the culture. When such forms naturally develop, they are unique treasures of the culture.

The Taj Mahal

At the apogee of the class of buildings displaying a unique form is the Taj Mahal (figure 9). This magnificent architectural essay is considered by many to be the most beautiful building in the world. It has come to be a lasting symbol for the Indian sub-continent in the minds of many people. The Taj Mahal was built by the Mughal Emperor Shah Jahan as a tomb for his wife Mumtaz Mahal following her death in 1631. His architect, Ustad Ahmad Lahori, was highly educated in engineering, mathematics, geometry, and the sciences of astronomy. So pleased was the emperor with the completed building that Shah Jahan awarded Ustad Ahmad

FIGURE 10. THE DISTINCTIVE GABLES OF LANDSHUT, BAVARIA.

the title Nadir-al-'Asr, or "Wonder of the Age." This domed building with its gleaming white marble and inlay of intricate colored stone motifs is an architectural triumph that succeeds in referencing traditional Mughal elements while fully developing a building form that is unique to India.

As is usually true of successful buildings, the Taj Mahal is a continuation of an existing building tradition within the culture and is a further development and perfection of an already existing type and form. Similar garden tombs for the emperors Humayun, Akbar, and Jahangir already existed or were under construction when Shah Jahan began work on the Taj Mahal. It appears that the Taj is most closely related in design to the tomb of Humayun completed in 1570, (figure 11) but is larger in scale and more perfect in its proportions and inlaid ornamentation. In its evolution of the garden tomb complex, the Taj Mahal introduces an innovation in the design of the complex by placing the tomb at one end of the garden rather than at the exact center, as had previously been the case (figure 63). This innovation may have been the result of a desire for the complex to be a more direct statement about the Islamic belief

Figure 11. Tomb of Humayun, Nizamuddin, New Delhi.

in an afterlife. According to W.E. Begley, "By adopting this unusual layout, the architect seems to have been inspired by a then well-known Islamic cosmological diagram depicting the garden of Paradise on the Day of Resurrection, in an apparent attempt to make each part of the tomb complex correspond allegorically to a celestial architectural model."[9] Thus, the Taj Mahal is more than likely a reflection of the widespread use of paradise imagery in both literature and art in the Mughal period through its thoughtfully conceived geometric layout. As such, it expresses Shah Jahan's hope in a future resurrection and the love he had for his wife, all in the tangible form of a building.

According to the Mughal histories of the building, the complex is laid out on a grid that is 400 Mughal yards wide and 1,050 Mughal yards long. A Mughal yard is believed to be the equivalent of 31.55 inches. As suggested by Begley, it also appears that the position and size of the buildings may have been determined by an overlaying grid of diagonal squares of 100 yards per side. The tomb is said to have been completed in six years while the garden, its monumental gate and accessory buildings are said to have required an additional five years. Given the challenges of building on the bank of a river and the resources in manpower and material required for such a great complex, the relatively short construction period is a remarkable testimony to the architect and his construction team.

The Taj Mahal's intricate ornamentation is a delight to the eye and is worthy of close study. It is of primary importance because the form and space of the building is more fully explained through it. Although the Koran does not specifically prohibit images of living creatures, Islamic architecture generally avoids such images and instead makes use of stylized vegetation, geometric patterns, and elaborate calligraphy. In the Taj Mahal, we find examples of all three of these incorporated in an aesthetically complementary form.

Figure 12. Calligraphy. Taj Mahal.

The two structural elements defining the form of the Taj Mahal are the arch and the dome. They are related because the dome has a profile similar to the arch and is therefore the solid counterpoint to the void of the arch. While Islamic architecture has a variety of pointed arch shapes, the keel-shaped arch (figure 13) is the dominant element of the Taj Mahal. The architect makes creative use of this arch by incorporating it in a number of ways. He sometimes encloses the arch within a rectangular border, which in turn is decorated with stylistically rendered calligraphy (figure 12). In other instances, he repeats the arch to create a pattern. The Taj Mahal masterfully exemplifies all of these features. The main portal is just such a keel-arch within a border filled with calligraphy. The effect is beautiful and inspirational at the same time. "The Taj Mahal clearly stands as the logical culmination of the earlier Mughal tradition, combining bold engineering and massive scale with formal elegance and a totally coordinated design of flawless visual symmetry."[10]

Opposite: Figure 13. Keel-shaped arch. Taj Mahal.

CHAPTER 2
THE CLASSICAL IDEAL

One of the great abuses of the term "classical" has been its exclusive application to the architecture of Western Europe to the exclusion of all others by certain architectural theorists. Yet, the architectural forms of Egypt, China, Indonesia, and the Indian sub-continent are just as worthy of being identified as "classic." This Western bias has had a detrimental effect on the architectural development of other world cultures. Some have believed these theorists and have emulated the West to the exclusion of fully developing their own indigenous style. While this is the path of least resistance, it is not the path that leads to variety and diversity, much less to a culturally rich architecture that ennobles a people and creates a unique sense of place. Therefore, we need to have a more complete understanding of the classical ideal and of the very definition of classicism itself.

Classicism Defined
Let us begin with the hypothesis that there is a larger classicism and a smaller classicism. In the larger sense, classicism is a state of perfection, as old and as new as architecture itself. When fully developed, it expresses an aesthetic truth that stands the test of time. Its methods are repeatable because its design principles are clear and definable. Classicism provides a connection to the past and is part of a building tradition that does not alienate a society from its culture or from Nature, but relates to both of them in all their depth. True classicism ennobles a society and enhances the dignity of its people.

In the smaller, more limited sense, classicism is commonly associated with the architecture of ancient Greece and Rome. This is usually represented by various columns and capitals known as Orders. These consist of the Tuscan, Doric, Ionic, Corinthian, and Composite (figure 14). While they were developed for use in Greek and Roman temple architecture, they have been adapted over the centuries by a number of cultures for use in a broad range of building types. Because of this adaptability and usefulness over the centuries, these Orders are considered to be "classic". It is this creative adaptation by architects over multiple generations that is the hallmark of classic architecture. This is the proof of a style's perfection.

The Role of Good Taste
There is in art and architecture a point of perfection as there is goodness or ripeness in Nature. People who train their eyes to discern proper scale, proportion, the rhythms of Nature, and fine ornament, can be said to have good taste; people who do not, and whose love falls short of it, can be said to have faulty taste. It is possible then to say that there is such a thing as good taste and bad taste, and we can make distinctions about tastes.[11] People are sometimes reluctant to voice an opinion on this topic out of a wrongly held belief that this matter is entirely of a personal nature and that no objective opinion can be rendered on the subject. There are some who go so far as to say that there are no standards regarding taste. Yet, if a culture adopts the premise that there are no absolutes or principles by which to make aesthetic judgments, then it opens itself up to many possible abuses by those architects and artists whose work is motivated by a desire to gain personal notoriety through vulgarity. Therefore, an understanding of the principles underlying aesthetics is necessary to adequately form judgments about the merits of a building's design.

Those who make judgments on matters of taste fall into three primary groups—individuals, academic and design professionals, and government leaders. As individuals, we each have the right to express our opinion about that which we deem to be beautiful. At an individual level, the aphorism: "Beauty lies in the eye of

Figure 14. Scamozzi's Five Orders. The Tuscan, Roman Doric, Ionic, Corinthian, and Composite orders after Scamozzi: (A) cornice, (B) frieze, (C) architrave, (D) capital, (E) shaft, (F) base, (G) cap or cornice, (H) die or dado, (I) plinth; (A), (B), (C) comprise the entablature; (D), (E), (F) the column; (G), (H), (I) the pedestal. Vincenzo Scamozzi, *L'idea della architettura universale*, Venice, 1615. Part II, Book 6, p. 6.

the beholder" stands true. Each of us will view things differently based on our education, temperament, and environment. However, the further a person's opinion strays from the basic principles underlying aesthetics, the more likely it is that he or she will stand alone in that opinion.

Those at the academic and professional level are the guardians of the basic principles of aesthetics. For better or for worse, this group is ultimately responsible for the talent available to a society since they have the critical responsibility of training and developing future practitioners. The potential for greatness is entirely dependent upon the educational system's ability to recognize talent, to nurture it through quality training, and to provide opportunities to put that talent into practice. Thus, this group's influence on matters of taste is of great significance.

Government leaders have historically had a major role in the commissioning of major public and private works. For most of mankind's history, monarchs and other ruling elite built every important building—the defining structures of their time. This fact is reflected in the names given to national architectural styles. These are named after the king or queen whose singular personality was closely related to the architecture built during their reign. There are many examples of this historic pattern in England alone. The Elizabethan/Tudor style was named for Elizabeth I; the Georgian style was named for buildings built during the consecutive reigns of George I, II, and III; the Regency style for that of George IV who was Regent before ascending the throne. Victorian architecture is associated with Queen Victoria's reign and Edwardian architecture with that of the reign of Edward VII.

The same pattern can be found in the architecture of France beginning with the reign of Louis XIV. The architecture of this period was closely associated with the Sun King and was known as the style *Louis Quatorze*. This close association of the architectural fashion of the day and the monarch continued after Louis' death in 1715 when the architecture during the years of his heir's minority was known as the *Regence style*.

The architectural fashion during the time of Louis XV was known as the style *Louis Quinze* and that during the reign of Louis XVI, which was characterized by an elegant neo-classicism, as the style *Louis Seize*.

Kings and their court set the tone and level of good taste for their nations by patronizing the best artists of their time and advancing the building trades through progressive building programs. Monarchs do this best when they are educated and sophisticated in taste, surrounding themselves with the very best talent the world has to offer. For example, Leonardo da Vinci was invited to leave Italy to serve in the French court at Avignon. Between the years 1660–1690, a group of Italian artists, including the architect and sculptor Bernini, was summoned to the court of Louis XIV; and in the last half of the 18th century, the Scottish architect Charles Cameron spent the better part of his professional career designing palaces for the Russian imperial family. These monarchs had developed informed opinions about taste and had the foresight and determination to search the world to find those individuals who could produce masterpieces to enhance their domains. It is through this sort of informed patronage that good taste can pervade the various aspects and trades associated with a society's built work.

The Role of Genius

When an architect or artist produces a work of great beauty and originality that advances the search for a new aestheticism, that work may be said to be the result of genius. That spark of genius, so unpredictable and unexpected, impossible to teach as a skill, is often the turning point for many cultures toward aesthetic greatness. Societies possessing persons of such talent are fortunate because genius is innate and cannot be learned. While the fundamentals of an art form can be taught and mastered, the person who goes on to exhibit an exceptional talent for that art does so because of a natural talent for which he or she already possesses an aptitude. It is present at birth and needs only to be awakened and nurtured to reveal itself. Research by the psychologist H.J. Eysenck

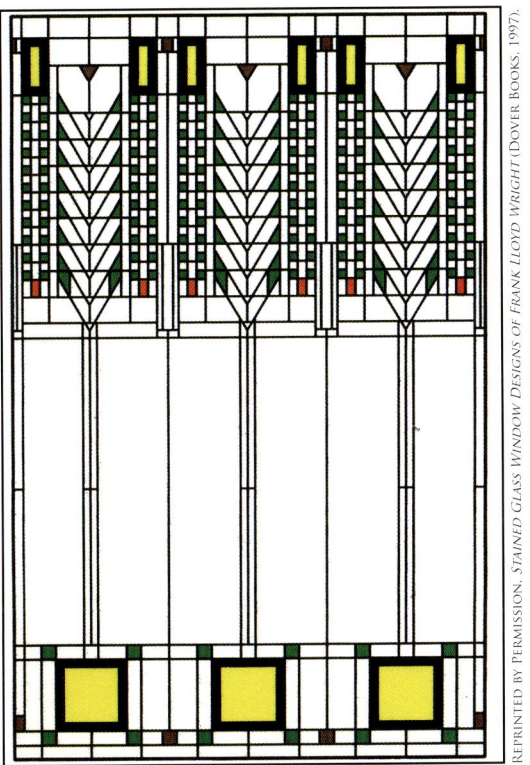

Figure 15. Leaded glass window, Martin House.

Figure 16. Leaded glass window, Dane House.

supports this hypothesis. He says, "there exists some property of the nervous system which determines aesthetic judgments, a property which is biologically derived. One deduction for instance, might be that this ability should be very strongly determined by heredity; there is already some evidence for this point of view."[12] It stands to reason then that, statistically speaking, every society should have their complement of persons endowed with a special aptitude for architectural design. Once these persons are identified, they can be provided with opportunities to develop and master their rare talent. The role of genius in architecture cannot be underestimated. Many of the great movements in world architecture were initiated by one man. In the 20th century, we saw such genius in the work of Frank Lloyd Wright.

Frank Lloyd Wright and the Prairie School of Architecture

Frank Lloyd Wright (1867–1959) is seldom associated with classicism, yet his work can serve as an excellent example of an original and fresh approach to design that works within the five principles for architectural excellence. One of the first observations about Wright's work is that there is little, if any, precedent for his architecture in America. His buildings are original, without prototype. They are born out of Wright's own genius, the early influence of his employment in the office of Louis Sullivan from 1887–93, and by his visit to Japan in 1905. In fact, he developed a love for Japanese art and published a book on Japanese woodcuts in 1912.[13] Over the years, Wright wrote numerous articles and books on his views of architectural theory.

Figure 17. Robie House, Chicago, Illinois.

Wright sets forth his agenda for residential design in his 1908 treatise *In the Cause of Architecture*. In it, he presents six principles for design: 1) simplicity and repose; 2) there should be as many kinds (styles) of houses as there are kinds of people; 3) a house should relate to its site and have a form that complements its surroundings; the prairie house should share the horizontality of the landscape, with gently sloping roofs, low proportions, quiet sky lines, suppressed, heavy set chimneys and sheltering overhangs; 4) its colors should conform to those of Nature; 5) the nature of the materials should be brought out; 6) a house of character will become more valuable with age.[14] Wright's residential work over the years faithfully reflected these principles.

His building forms and ornamentation were at once new yet understandable within their larger American context. As Wright was designing his unique houses, he developed a new vocabulary that permeated his work and set it apart as a distinct style. The horizontal lines, the low or flat-pitched roofs, wide steel reinforced cantilevered balconies, linear brickwork, and distinctive leaded windows were new elements of style to American residential architecture. Over time, his architecture came to be known as the Prairie School.

The Prairie School was born in the American Midwest and referenced the materials and colors familiar to the people of the plains states. It was considered to be avant-garde for its time and received a positive response from independent minded midwesterners. During this period, Americans were taking a sentimental look back at the culture of the Plains Indians, which was quickly becoming a distant memory. Wright's decorative motifs may have drawn upon the textile patterns found in American Indian weaving for their inspiration. This can best be observed in the geometric patterns of his leaded glass windows with their arrow and chevron motifs (figures 15–16). Leaded windows were commonly used in houses of all types during this period, but Wright's were unique in their design and they became a recognizable feature of his houses.

One house that best exemplifies many of his early design innovations is the Robie House (1908–10) located in a suburb south of Chicago, Illinois (figure 17). According to Karen A. Sweeney, AIA, Director of Restoration for the Frank Lloyd Wright Preservation Trust, "Wright viewed it as his ultimate Prairie house. He was actively involved in saving it twice."[15] The Robie House introduces many new features unknown in American residential design of the time. First of all, the plan itself is revolutionary in its location of the entry, which is not readily apparent from the street. The home's entry is hidden behind a privacy wall and is at a 90-degree angle to the street. This is in contrast to the typical home of the time, which presented its entry as the central feature of the front façade. Secondly, the floor plan is "open" as opposed to a series of individually connected rooms. In this respect, Wright was a generation ahead of his time. The plan also included a number of advances in planning that would not appear in the typical American home for years. One of these was the home's attached three-car garage.

Stylistically, the Robie House reflects all the design elements upon which Wright built his reputation. The house features broad roof overhangs, linear brickwork accented by horizontal bands of limestone, Wright's distinctive leaded glass work, bold decorative accents like the oversized urns on the front privacy wall, and massive chimneys which punctuate the roof near its center, providing balance and visual lift to counterbalance the house's strong horizontal lines. In addition to the house's plan and stylistic innovations, Wright incorporated the latest technological advances of the time including a central vacuum system and electrically illuminated leaded glass panels along the perimeter of the living room and dining room ceilings. As such, the Robie House serves as a wonderful example of the new and creative architecture represented by Wright and his Prairie School architecture.

Wright's most famous house, Fallingwater, (figure 18) is often called the greatest American house of the 20th century. It was built in 1936 for Pittsburgh industrialist Edgar Kauffman as a weekend "cottage" and fits into the landscape and complements the natural beauty of the site. Wright said of his approach to a building's design in relation to its site, "We start with the ground, in any and every case the character of the site is the beginning of the building that aspires to architecture. All must begin where they stand."[16] Fallingwater's cantilevered terraces of reinforced concrete project out from the rock base, appearing to float out over the water, as if unsupported. The horizontal lines, flat roof, and use of stucco and native stone continue Wright's interest in blending his work with its environment. "It is in the nature of any organic building," says Wright, "to grow from its site, come out of the ground into the light—the ground itself held always as a basic component part of the building itself."[17] Furthering the house's connection with its natural surroundings was Wright's use of steel casement windows, which extend to the corners of the rooms. These special windows open up the otherwise solid corners to allow for better views of the stream and wooded hills. These windows with their red frames lend an airy feel to the space. Their pattern is much simpler than those of his early career and reflects the style of fenestration that would soon be favored by the International School. Fallingwater's most prominent feature is its cantilevered porch, which overhangs the stream running alongside the house.

Figure 18. Fallingwater, Mill Run, Pennsylvania.

An engineering marvel for its time, it made use of structural steel for its support and created the look of a floating balcony. Fallingwater received immediate international acclaim and is still considered a masterpiece three-quarters of a century after it was built. Thus, time is verifying the opinion that the house is an enduring classic.

Can we identify in Wright's work the five underlying principles of architectural excellence? Does it reference a past tradition? In some respect, Wright successfully creates his own tradition and reference point, and in architecture this is rare. However, Wright's Prairie School of architecture does allude to the cultural motifs of the Midwest Plains Indians and in this respect it connects with an understood past to some extent. His work may also reference the art of Japan, which was enjoying a revival of interest in America during this time. What about its ability to be rationally understood or codified? His principles for massing and ornamentation are identifiable and repeatable by others. His strong horizontal lines, cantilevers, and window treatments all became identified with the Prairie Style. In fact, many architects have successfully repeated buildings in Wright's style, and this demonstrates its ability to be rationally understood. What about it being sympathetic to the rhythms of Nature? Wright's highly developed sense of design is sympathetic to those elements that connect his work to the rhythms, sequences, and symmetry and asymmetry found in Nature. What about his materials? Wright was one of the first architects to choose native stone and colors that deliberately blended with the surrounding land. As a result, his houses often appear to be an extension of the land. Because his work meets these key principles and has endured over time, especially in the American Midwest, it can be said to demonstrate true excellence.

CHAPTER 3
TRADITION AS THE BASIS FOR DESIGN

Architecture of excellence is able to reference past traditions found within the collective memory of its culture, thus providing a touchstone to a shared past. Such architecture evokes a common understanding and emotional response. Architecture inspired by tradition helps national, regional, and local groups preserve or even develop their uniqueness in the larger world community. Architecture that references tradition celebrates a culture's history, thus preserving it for future generations. This, in turn, enriches a society by giving it a unique sense of cultural identity and community. The essence of tradition consists of more than *style*. Tradition is the accumulated wisdom of proven ways of seeing and doing. Architecture based on tradition draws upon the best from the past and reinterprets it for the present. It is not a fossilized version of what has come before. Rather, architecture is a living language that constantly adapts itself to new circumstances and functional needs in inventive ways. This is what it means to be *modern* in the best sense of the word.

Tradition provides a fresh look at established norms and creates an architecture that is a proper reflection of the needs of its time. The 20th-century architect Charles Warren McAllister has said that in order for tradition to retain its potency and pertinence, "each generation has to remake, so to speak, its own image of the past in the perspective of its own problems. Tradition then is a convenient, if vague, term for the process whereby a generation uses valid elements of its inheritance to be interpreted for its own purpose. The problem is to strike a balance, without compromising either, between relevant tradition and essential innovation."[18]

Novelty and the Bizarre
Architectural novelty based on the bizarre is the antithesis of design excellence. The bizarre makes no reference to a common past, thus making no effort to invoke feelings or memories of a shared cultural experience. While the bizarre succeeds in getting attention, it does not contribute to a society's journey toward developing its own architecture of excellence. Buildings based on the bizarre are more often the product of an architect's desire to self-promote rather than an act of creating something of real architectural merit and longevity. The architect Harry Weese made this same point when he said, "Virtuoso performances receive acclaim. If an architect produces a tour de force defying gravity, it is bound to attract attention. But unless the work becomes part of the stream of development, it is meaningless."[19]

Tradition is a critical element that cannot be marginalized or ignored in the creation of architecture. Tradition is the essential element that allows a new work to connect with people on an emotional and intellectual level. The recollection of the familiar is one aspect of design that produces pleasure. This feeling of pleasure or satisfaction exists because we enjoy a sense of security among things that we know and understand.[20] References to a previous tradition are a common component of most major architectural movements. While these movements utilized new technologies, building materials, or invented new building forms, each evoked an emotional response having its roots in an earlier tradition. Perhaps by examining some of the more dominant movements, we can find inspiration for new ways in which tradition can be a contributing component of the architecture of our own time and place.

Tradition in Greek Architecture
It is speculated that Greek temples are interpretations in stone of an earlier tradition of buildings that were made of wood. While none of the earlier structures have been preserved, it is thought that these were of post and beam

Figure 19. Illustrations of proposed wooden temple construction. Giovanantonio Rusconi, *Della Architettura*, 1590.

construction fastened with wooden dowels or pegs. Many of the details found on Greek temples seem to echo earlier wooden construction techniques in their various stone details (figure 19). The horizontal stonework resting upon the column is the *entablature* and consists of three parts: the *architrave*, *frieze*, and *cornice* (figure 20). The architrave rests directly upon the column, as would have a wooden beam, and carries the load of that which is directly above it. Its weight bearing function is expressed through the simple horizontal lines, or projecting faces of the architrave. Above the architrave rests the frieze. This band with its grooved and doweled *triglyphs* seems to represent the ends of the wooden roof beams that would have rested on the architrave. The ends of the triglyphs are decorated with vertical V-shaped notches with fastening dowels beneath. The intermediary spaces between the triglyphs are referred to as *metopes*. In some instances, as on the Parthenon, these metopes are decorated with sculpture (figure 21). Above the frieze rests the cornice, which is related to the support of the roofing tiles. This function is expressed by its projecting profile, which in turn sheds rainwater from the face of the building. Thus, these stone temples may be incorporating design elements from earlier temples of wood even though these details no longer had any real function. Instead, recalling the traditions of the earlier temples, these details were retained by the architect to serve a purely decorative role. These new stone temples were a dignified and beautiful solution to the problem of more

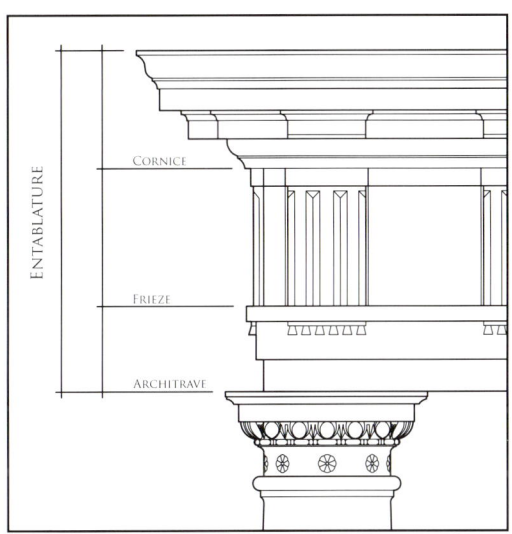

Figure 20. Illustration of an entablature.

Figure 21. Metopes, The Parthenon.

permanently housing their gods using the more durable material of stone. Yet, at the same time, these temples referenced familiar details that announced the building's purpose and heritage. The finest example of a temple incorporating all of these elements is the Parthenon, located on the Acropolis in Athens, Greece.

The Parthenon

The temple of Athena Polias, or the Parthenon, was built during the golden age of Athenian art (447–438 B.C.) and was designed by the Greek architects Ictinus and Callicrates. The sculptural groups that adorn its pediments were carved by Phidias and his school. The Parthenon represents the height of Greek artistic achievement and stands today as one of the supreme examples of Greek architecture (figure 22). The building illustrates Greek mythological traditions and displays the evolutionary advancement of Greek temple design. The Parthenon's sculptural groups are essays in stone of well-known Greek myths. These are portrayed on the stone reliefs of its frieze and in the sculptural groups once located on its two pediments. The sculptures of the east pediment portray the birth of the goddess Athena, fully grown and completely armored. Nike comes forward to crown Athena with a laurel wreath, the symbol of victory. The corners of the pediment are anchored by Helios, the sun god, rising out of the left corner representing the break of day, and by Selene, the moon goddess, on the right corner representing evening. The west pediment (figure 23) illustrates the contest between Athena and Poseidon for the patronage of Attica and its capital city of Athens. In this contest, Poseidon strikes the rock of the Acropolis with his trident and brings forth salt water. Athena strikes the rock with her spear and an olive tree springs forth. The people of Athens preferred the gift of Athena to that of Poseidon and chose her as their patron goddess, naming their city in her honor. As put by Percy Gardner, a classical archeologist, "In celebrating the birth and victory of their goddess, the Athenians glorified their city; and in recording the exploits of their ancestry, they glorified Athena. Patriotism and religion were but two phases of the same feelings and aspirations."[21] Thus, the Parthenon embraces tradition, celebrates it, and enhances it through the storytelling of its sculpture.

The Parthenon also stands as the perfection of a traditional building type that was developed over centuries. It transcends what came before and establishes a unique place for itself in

Figure 23. Reproduction of the west pediment, Parthenon, Nashville, Tennessee.

the annals of architecture. In perfecting the Parthenon's design, the architects used subtle optical adjustments that refined earlier Greek experiments with temple design. While the architects may have used geometry and mathematics as a starting point, they nevertheless adjusted the resulting rigid correctness to the eye of the beholder. This dynamic nature of Greek architecture is the reason why it is generally considered to have more character, more life, than later Roman work. For example, the architects adjusted the building's stepped base so that it bends toward the building's four corners. All the outer columns lean inward toward the structure and the four corner columns lean inward diagonally. This inward tilt is so subtle that the vanishing points of their axes meet approximately 1.5 miles above the building. Furthermore, optical adjustments occur in the length of the building in the upward curve of the entablature, the reduction of column spacing at the end bays of the colonnade, and in the thickening of the end columns. The architects wanted the temple to look as if it were constructed upon a flat platform but were aware that if constructed thus it would appear to sag in the center. This effect was countered by curving the platform upward toward the center so that the Parthenon's midpoint is several inches higher than the outer edges of the platform. Similarly, the columns have a slight entasis, or bulge, to offset the concave effect in columns with perfectly straight sides. The geometric method the architects used to lay out the tapering of the columns is unknown, but it may have been an enormous segment of a circle rather than the method of tapering used later by the Romans.

These adjustments demonstrate the architects' mastery of their art, their visual sophistication, and the freedom they employed in the visual perfection of the Parthenon's aesthetics. Because of the splendid success achieved through these many optical adjustments, Western architecture was advanced, and the record of these subtleties was preserved in stone for rediscovery by future generations of architects. Ictinus and Callicrates incorporated traditional elements and adjusted them to create a unique sense of style that added to the living architecture of their own time. In this way, they honored previous Greek traditions while furthering their culture's artistic achievements. Their aesthetic advancements would eventually be rediscovered and enter the canon of Western architecture, while the Parthenon itself would come to represent that which is best in classical Greek architecture.

Tradition in Roman Architecture

The Romans were great innovators. Their contributions to architecture include the development of the arch and dome and the mastery of concrete. They were expert in building large and complicated projects. The ruins of their forums, amphitheaters, palaces, aqueducts, and coliseums found around the Mediterranean basin are broken reminders of the glory that was once Rome's. And yet, despite their innovative spirit, they consciously looked back to the architectural traditions of Greece in the design of their buildings. Roman architecture, with its columns, capitals, and friezes, directly references the architectural traditions of Greece. By doing so, Rome was associating itself with the cultural legacy of a neighboring people while declaring itself heir to the ideals and intellectual heritage of Greece. However, Roman architects reinterpreted these earlier prototypes and created their own unique classical tradition. The culmination of Rome's many contributions to architecture through its innovative building forms and construction technology can be found in one building—the Pantheon.

The Roman Pantheon

Hadrian's Pantheon (figure 24) encloses one of antiquity's most awe-inspiring spaces of light and void that symbolically represents in its architecture the imagined form of the universe. The Pantheon's bold monumental dome encloses a circular worship space and represents the summation of ideas developed by Roman architects and engineers (figure 25). Built to honor the pantheon of Roman gods, it combines arch and dome with traditional architectural elements to create a building honoring Rome's religious traditions while utilizing advanced Roman engineering and building materials.

Following pages: Figure 24. The Pantheon. Rome. Italy.

Figure 25. Interior view of the Pantheon, Rome, Italy.

In contrast to most religious architecture, the Pantheon's religious overtones are neutral. Because of this, the Pantheon attained a universality that transcends the city of Rome and relates to a broader world audience. It left a lasting influence on the architecture of Western civilization, perhaps more than any other building, inspiring architects of private residences and numerous churches. Today, when visitors pass through its ancient bronze doors and behold the great rotunda for the first time, the universal symbolism communicated by its domed enclosure still transcends time and space. Yet the Pantheon, for all its originality, is a building firmly rooted in the established traditions of the Rome of its time.

While the architect of the Pantheon is not known, it is believed the Emperor Hadrian was involved in its concept and was undoubtedly the motivating influence for its construction. Drawing upon the accumulated knowledge of Rome's remarkable engineering prowess, the architects of the Pantheon created a new building type that is at once novel and respectful of Rome's classical tradition. Its Corinthian columns, monumental temple-front portico, and classical entablature would have been immediately familiar to the Romans of the time. The Pantheon exhibits all the characteristics of design excellence. It is a building combining traditional architectural elements with a form that is sympathetic to the scale, proportions, rhythms, and symmetry of Nature. It is a building with functional utility that incorporates advanced engineering and durable materials. The Pantheon is a building that has stood the test of time. This is the ideal that architecture strives to achieve.

Tradition of Excellence in Chinese Architecture

Other societies have been equally successful in developing a memorable architecture that uniquely represents their culture. The people of China developed and perfected a lacquered wood and glazed tile architecture that singularly defined their society for hundreds of years. China's architectural vocabulary shows great versatility in meeting various functional needs.

Traditional Chinese architecture successfully combines distinctive elements such as flared rooflines, complex post and beam construction, or the use of red, white, yellow, and blue color schemes. While China has numerous examples of buildings that might be considered definitive examples, the palace complex in Beijing, known as the Forbidden City, contains the largest collection of classic Chinese architecture.

The Forbidden City, Beijing, China
Begun in the early 15th century and completed over generations, the Forbidden City (figure 27) is made up of dozens of buildings enclosed within a vast walled complex. The Forbidden City offers a glimpse of the infinite variety and diversity that is possible within an established genre of architectural thought. In addition to its traditional architectural forms, the Forbidden City's architecture incorporates traditional Chinese numerical and ornamental symbolism in its plan and ornamental details. Odd numbers were preferred for good luck with the number nine reserved for use by the emperor. There are nine rows of brass fasteners on the imperial gate (figure 26) and only buildings used by the emperor were allowed to have nine mythical beast figures on the ridges of the roof. Less important buildings have fewer of these figures but still in an odd number. Buildings within the Forbidden City have an odd number of rooms for good luck with the exception of the imperial library, which has six. Since the number six is associated with water, it was hoped that fire might be repulsed in this manner. Upon closer examination, one finds delightful variety among the many glazed roof tile designs and their related end caps. The roof charms, or roof-figures, only appear on imperial buildings (figure 28). These small glazed ceramic figures are typically arranged along the lower edge of the flared rooflines in an outward marching procession. The procession is led by a man riding a phoenix and is concluded by an imperial dragon at the end.

The phoenix and the dragon, as well as the mythical beasts in between (always in an odd number), had rich symbolic meanings for the Chinese court. The imperial dragon represents

Figure 26. Imperial gate, Forbidden City, Beijing, China.

the authority of the State, while the figure of the man riding the phoenix is traditionally associated with immortality or one of the immortal guardians of Chinese lore. The number of the mythical beasts indicates the status of the duties performed within the building or courtyard beyond the gate. The one exception to this rule of nine is found on the Hall of Supreme Harmony. Here there are ten mythical roof figures, the tenth being an image of an immortal holding a sword as if it were a walking stick.

The Forbidden City makes extensive use of fine materials as seen in its carved marble staircases and bronze ornaments and sculpture (figure 29). The imperial staircases, with their white marble panels of snarling dragons, are masterpieces

Following pages: Figure 27. Forbidden City, Beijing, China.

Figure 28. Roof charms, Forbidden City, Beijing, China.

Figure 29. Bronze lion, Forbidden City.

of the stone carver's art. Hardly any surface is left without some thoughtful ornamentation of carved detail (figures 30–32). In each of these, the artist was referencing a known tradition that was understandable within the context of the culture. Painters, silk weavers, and workers in bronze further enhanced the buildings with their magnificent artistry, creating a complete whole that fully represented the majesty and dignity of the emperor and his court. Throughout this enormous complex, tradition is honored and celebrated in the architecture and art of these magnificent buildings. As a result, the Forbidden City expresses a consistency that is a powerful reminder of the stability and dignity of the Chinese court of that era.

Tradition in the Architecture of the European Renaissance

The term "renaissance" means to be reborn or to rediscover. Beginning in 14th-century Italy, this new architectural movement would have widespread influence and last far into the 17th century. Taking inspiration from the architectural vocabulary of ancient Rome and

Figure 30. Glazed tile dragon. Forbidden City.

Figure 31. Marble mythological animal. Forbidden City.

Figure 32. Stone dragon. Forbidden City.

Greece, Renaissance architects looked to the past and reinterpreted it in their new building types. By doing so, they were drawing upon a cultural past that their society understood and admired. Proponents of an architecture based on earlier traditions found in Greece and Rome included the Italian architects Alberti, Palladio, Barbaro, Scamozzi, and others of their contemporaries. Each of these architects drew inspiration from Marcus Vitruvius Pollio's *De architectura* (translated as *The Ten Books on Architecture*). While we know little of Vitruvius' work as an architect of imperial Rome, his fame was assured by the fact that his *Ten Books* is the only detailed guide of Roman building design and engineering techniques to have been passed down to the modern world. In the 15th century, a reliable copy of Vitruvius' manuscript was discovered in the monastic library of St. Gallen, Switzerland and this copy, in turn, was sent to Florence for translation and illustration. Even though Vitruvius wrote this architectural treatise in the 1st century B.C., it became an architectural guide of great importance to Renaissance architects. Vitruvius' work during this later period reached a level of influence that he could hardly have imagined from his Roman-era perspective. This unusual case of delayed success was best explained by Herbert Koch who said, "In the history of art there is probably no other example of a systematic textbook aiming at contemporary influence, missing its target, and yet achieving such overwhelming success centuries after its appearance."[22] For Renaissance architects such as Alberti, the ancient orders described by Vitruvius, "stir us up by their instructions to produce something of our own invention and to endeavor to acquire equal or greater praise than they did."[23]

With the decline of the Roman Empire, the architectural concepts and instructions of Vitruvius were gradually forgotten. Byzantine and Romanesque buildings became more massive and ponderous, ignoring the elegant beauty of their Roman legacy. Gradually though, there began to be a renewed interest in the classical ruins of Rome and the building technology that made these buildings possible. This interest in Roman architecture would come to be more fully studied and described by one of Italy's own sons, Andrea Palladio.

Andrea Palladio

Called "the most imitated architect in history," Andrea di Pietro della Gondola (1508–1580), later called "Palladio," (figure 33) is one of the first influential Renaissance architects to make significant use of the classical orders since the fall of ancient Rome. Palladio was both a scholar and an antiquarian. He was one of the first of his generation to go to Rome to study the ancient ruins with sketchbook and measuring rod in hand. While the doctrine for classical architecture had been somewhat developed, or codified, in the 1st century B.C. by the Roman architect Vitruvius, its tenets had been largely forgotten until an edition was published in 1550, illustrated with drawings by Palladio. In 1554, Palladio published two books of his own. The first described the antiquities of Rome while the second described its churches. But it was his

Figure 33. Francesco Zucchi (1692–1764), Palladio, Ashmoleou Museum, Oxford, Engraving, 15.8 x 10.1. Bruce Boucher and Andrea Palladio, *The Architect in His Time* (New York: Abbeville Press, 1998).

final work, the *I Quattro libri dell'architettura*, or *The Four Books of Architecture*, published in 1570 that was to change the course of Western architecture. This book is primarily responsible for the reintroduction of classical architectural vocabulary into the buildings of Western civilization.

Palladio followed the Vitruvian principle that perfection in architecture is best achieved when buildings fulfill the principles of beauty, permanence, and commodity. Renaissance architects believed they could accomplish these three goals by following the proportions, rhythm, scale, and symmetry found in Nature. Through examples illustrated in his book, Palladio proposed that architecture should make use of the proportions found in the human body and thus achieve a divine perfection. Like his contemporaries in painting and sculpture, Palladio believed the human form was the key to perfect harmony since man was "formed in the image of God." Establishing the human body as a divine model, Renaissance architects strove to achieve a balance and perfection in their buildings that have, in Palladio's own words, "a correspondence of the whole to all the parts, of the parts to each other, and of those parts to the whole."[24] It was also during the 16th century that a standard module of measurement, the 12-inch foot, was adopted to aid in the translation of proportions from the human body to the design of a building. He further states that in the design of a building, the basic services should be hidden according to the principles found in the parts of the body, so that the most beautiful should be in places exposed to sight and the less decent in hidden places.[25] Until the rupture within traditional building design that occurred in the 20th century, this concept of appropriateness was taken for granted as common sense by all.

Palladio's first important opportunity to demonstrate his mastery of classical design came when he received a commission to remodel the municipal building in his hometown of Vicenza, Italy. This dark brick Gothic-style building dated from the Middle Ages and consisted of a patchwork of buildings that served as a multi-

FIGURE 34. BASILICA, VICENZA, ITALY.

purpose building for municipal functions. It was a tremendous challenge and Palladio's solution transformed the building into a magnificent essay in Roman classicism (figure 34). His success in this endeavor brought him, and the revival of Roman classicism, international acclaim. Soon, governments all over Europe desired to have similar buildings enhancing their cities. Palladio's success was the architectural announcement that the Middle Ages were over and that the ideals of the Renaissance had triumphed.

Palladio demonstrated that the architectural traditions of ancient Rome could be adapted to the design of a diverse range of building types. With almost 50 villas, palaces, civic buildings, and churches to his credit, he never directly copied antiquity but reinterpreted it for his own new use. Though intimately familiar with Vitruvius, he used Vitruvian rules only when it served his purpose. Three of Palladio's buildings have proven to be particularly influential on Western building design. These buildings are La Rotunda, Villa Malcontenta, and Il Redentore (figures 35–37). These three buildings have served as prototypes for countless buildings around the world. Palladio's influence can be seen in the many creative adaptations of his principles in buildings ranging from capitols to private homes. Architects from many nations came to Italy to study Palladio's work and returned to their home countries to interpret his work in their own way. Two examples in England include Queen's House (1618–35) by Inigo Jones (figure 38) and Chiswick House (1729) by Lord Burlington (figure 39). An important example in the United States is Monticello (1768–1809) located in Charlottesville, Virginia. In this, his personal home, gentleman architect and statesman Thomas Jefferson incorporated Palladian motifs, a classical portico, and Roman dome to create one of America's architectural treasures (figure 40).

Figure 35. La Rotunda, Vicenza, Italy, 1566–67.

Figure 36. Villa Malcontenta, near Venice, Italy, 1559–60.

Figure 37. Il Redentore, Venice, Italy, 1576–92.

Figure 38. Queen's House, Greenwich, England.

Figure 39. Chiswick House, Richmond, England.

Figure 40. Monticello, Charlottesville, Virginia.

Figure 41. Oval salon, Hôtel de Soubise, Paris, France, 1735.

Tradition in French Neo-Classicism

Architecture has always been in the forefront of the many arts produced by France. The architectural tradition of France has been a distinguished one. The first manifestation of its genius occurred in the Gothic movement, its second was the development of neo-classicism in the second half of the 18th century. This neo-classical period was a time when France looked back to the *grand siecle* of Louis XIV and the classical buildings of Greece and Rome to find inspiration for its development of pervasive new design aesthetics. This revival affected all aspects of French design, not just its architecture. It influenced the design of furnishings and fashions, the nation's city planning, and even the design of municipal structures such as bridges.

As is often the case in the development of an architectural movement, French neo-classicism evolved in reaction to that which had preceded it—the florid excesses of Rococo and the society of the time with its perceived decadences. In its day, Rococo was known as the *style picturesque* (figure 41). It only came to be called Rococo, derived from the French word *rocaille* meaning rocky or irregular ground, as a derogative term in the mid-19th century. The Rococo abandoned all the established rules and orders and adopted a fluidity that culminated in an architecture of C-curves, stylized flowers, palm trees, shell motifs, and stylized rock formations—hence the name Rococo. It was the eventual public reaction against Rococo that laid the groundwork for the revival of a more traditionally based architecture. Oddly enough, it was not nostalgia for antiquity that drove the neo-classical movement, but rather nostalgia for France's more recent past. It was believed at the time that Rococo, for all its exuberance, was still in some way inferior to the architecture from the time of Louis XIV half a century earlier.

Two contemporary experts, Blondel and Voltaire, expressed the opinion that the architecture of the previous generation was superior to that of the Rococo movement. Blondel's essay on architecture for Diderot's *Encyclopédie* [26] expresses this thought while Voltaire speaks of the perfection of the arts during the reign of Louis XIV in his *Histoire de Louis XIV* (1751). They shared the opinion that the architecture of the earlier period had been one of the apogees of human history. Seeing the Rococo movement as ultimately a degenerate style, the public began to have a renewed interest in France's more classical architectural traditions. The architecture of the last half of the 18th century therefore consciously referenced the architectural traditions of the previous century and even further back to the architecture of Vignola, Palladio, and Scamozzi, and ultimately to that of ancient Greece and Rome. There was a general opinion that this earlier classicism represented higher moral values and was more closely aligned with the Enlightenment and its ideals. Thus, France led much of Europe in a return to the previous traditions of symmetry, straight lines, columns, pilasters, and other classical motifs (figure 42). Most importantly, while the buildings of this neo-classical movement make full use of the classical orders, the revival created new buildings in both form and type that are distinctly different from those that had come before. In the spirit of architectural excellence, these buildings take inspiration from earlier traditions to create an architecture that is entirely new. Thus, the buildings of the French neo-classical movement remained true to the character of French culture while expressing an entirely fresh aesthetic.

Following pages: Figure 42. Place de la Concorde. Paris. France.

Figure 43. King's state bedroom, Royal Palace, Stockholm, Sweden.

Tradition in Swedish Neo-Classicism

The neo-classicism that began in France swept through Europe in the late 18th century with each country interpreting the movement in its own way. Rather than merely copying these French prototypes, Swedish designers reinterpreted them into the national aesthetic of their country. They excelled in creating a neo-classicism that captured the expression of Swedish sensibilities. The architecture built at this time demonstrates how the principles of architectural excellence can guide the design of buildings while allowing the spirit of the culture to express itself.

Crown Prince Gustav was on a study trip in Paris in 1771 when he learned of his father's death. He returned to Sweden as Gustav III and brought back with him a first-hand understanding of the French neo-classical style, which was just then starting to dominate European design. It was during his 20-year reign as a sophisticated patron of the arts that neo-classicism was nurtured and flourished into something uniquely Swedish. Aiding Gustav in his desire to create beautiful buildings and interiors were two Swedish architects, Carl Fredrik Adelcrantz and Jean Eric Rehn. Drawing upon their own study trips to France and the architectural publications and engravings of the time, Adelcrantz and Rehn created many of the buildings and interiors we admire today. It was Rehn who decorated Gustav's State Bedroom in the Royal Palace in

Figure 44. Swedish interior, Haga Pavilion, Stockholm, Sweden.

Stockholm (figure 43). This room, considered to be the first Swedish neo-classical interior, was created in 1772. The state bedroom, with its bed alcove, gilded baluster, decoratively painted ceiling adorned with putti, and classical detailing, shows Gustav's admiration for the latest designs coming from France. Seeing in French culture a sophistication that Sweden lacked, Gustav adopted this movement with enthusiasm, transforming his country and leaving a strong architectural legacy that is still a source of pride to Sweden today.

Characteristic of the architecture of Sweden during this time is a restraint unseen in the architecture of France and Germany during the same period. Swedish architects made use of pilasters, columns, and classical entablatures in their buildings, but their interiors are characterized by a restrained simple elegance (figure 44). Furthermore, these interiors make use of pale grays and whites, picked out with the lightest touches of gold combined with delicately painted canvas work, lending the interiors a lightness that provides a welcomed relief from the long dark winters of Sweden's northern climate. The architecture of Gustav's reign came to be known as the *Gustavian Style* and, as such, is a successful expression of Sweden's national aesthetic values while working within the broader principles of architectural excellence.

Tradition in the English Arts and Crafts Movement

As with most great movements, the memory of some previous tradition serves as the underlying inspiration. This was true for the English Arts and Crafts Movement. Deep within the collective memory of the English people was a fond and distant memory of the Gothic period and its unique architecture. This revival of the Gothic had its beginning in the later part of the 18th century in the construction and reconstruction of a number of picturesque country houses. Taking up the new style and developing it further was Augustus Welby Northmore Pugin (1812–1852). Pugin was a prodigy and a prodigious designer whose entire short career (he died at 40 from "exhaustion") was devoted to the 19th-century interpretation of the Gothic. Pugin was already recognized as a great talent by his teenage years. His first major commission, at the age of 15, came when he was asked to design Gothic-style furniture to complement Sir Jeffry Wyatville's reconstruction of Windsor castle in 1827. Following this success, Pugin founded a firm specializing in the design of Gothic-style building components for application to the surface of finished buildings. He excelled in producing faithful replicas of medieval pieces and found a ready market for his work. Despite his short career, Pugin was instrumental in

Figure 45. Houses of Parliament, London, England.

laying the foundation upon which the Arts and Crafts Movement would more broadly capture the public's imagination within a few years of his death.

By the middle of the 19th century, the Gothic had become the preferred style for churches and a number of other kinds of buildings. One of the most notable of these was the new Houses of Parliament built in an idealized form of Gothic (figure 45). At this time, the English Industrial Revolution was in full force. The result was the demise of many small cottage industries that were unable to compete with the mass production of items previously made by hand. The Arts and Crafts Movement was born as a reaction to this situation. More philosophical in nature than an actual stylistic school of design with defined principles, the Arts and Crafts Movement was concerned with the revival of traditional English hand crafts.

Its chief proponent, William Morris (1834–1896), was the founder of the Arts and Crafts Exhibition Society. Although he did not found the Society until 1888, Morris had been actively designing and writing to promote his new and original approach to design for the previous two decades. Morris advocated an individualistic view toward design and craftsmanship that

Figure 46. Deanery Gardens, Edwin Luytens, architect.

valued simplicity, truth of materials, and local craftsmanship and design. The movement drew its inspiration from the traditions of England's Gothic period rather than the classicism of Greece and Rome. This period of the nation's architectural history was seen as being less affected by foreign influence and more true to the English spirit. This was a reaction to the architecture of the previous decade that had witnessed the popularity of the Italianate style. Ultimately, however, the English public came to reject the Italianate style as foreign. The timing was just right for Morris' school of thought, and the English public eagerly adopted the Arts and Crafts style.

Although Morris never designed any architecture, his influence was felt throughout England. There were a number of architects, however, who did design buildings following the tenets of the Arts and Crafts Movement. Among these were Edwin Luytens and C.F.A. Voysey (figures 46–47). These architects found an appreciative public for this style of building and continued to design them well into the early 20th century. Their buildings share Morris's love of simplicity and a free, less academic, feel for the Gothic. These buildings are characterized by their somewhat austere appearance that is often void of superfluous detail. They rely on their asymmetrical massing, simply treated flat planes, and crisp edged window and roof rake details to achieve their overall effect.

Figure 47. The Hill, C.F.A. Voysey, architect.

CHAPTER 4
RATIONALISM AS THE BASIS FOR DESIGN

In order for a new architectural movement to enter the canon of a culture, it must be understood rationally so other designers can repeat it. This is a key point. Architecture is at its best when it has definable mathematic or geometric relationships as well as a clear ornamental vocabulary. If it has such, then architects can emulate it and perpetuate it beyond the originator. Thus, reason is an essential component of excellence in design. As the great theologian Thomas Aquinas (1225–1274) said, "Reason is the first principle of all human work."[27] It is precisely because the architecture of ancient Greece and Rome can be described using rational means that they have enjoyed such long use. Rational descriptions allow architecture from one time and place to be adapted to other forms and types of buildings in a totally different context. Furthermore, the simpler these rational principles are the better. Even an expert in another field of study such as the physicist Schrödinger (1887–1961) proposed that, "The creative vigor of a general principle depends precisely on its generality."[28] The French mathematician and architect Roland Fréart de Chambray (1606–1676) expresses the same thought, "For the excellence and perfection of an art does not consist in the multiplicity of its principles; on the contrary, the simpler and fewer these are, the more is art to be admired: and this we see in the rules of Geometry, which is the basis and general font of all the arts…"[29]

By developing a rational system to describe architecture, the professional is creating a language by which others may emulate his or her work. The architecture of Greece and Rome

FIGURE 48. FIGURE OF DORIC COLUMN, JOHN SHUTE, *THE FIRST AND CHIEF GROUNDS OF ARCHITECTURE*, 1563, VI.

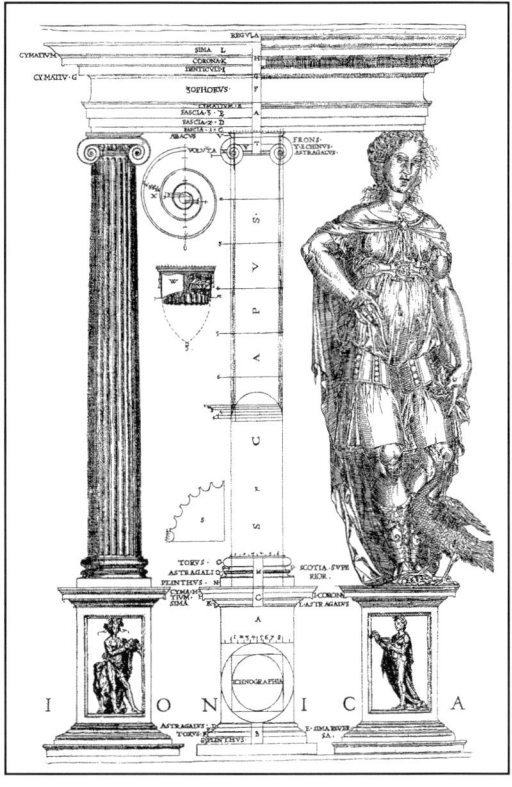

FIGURE 49. FIGURE OF IONIC COLUMN, JOHN SHUTE, *THE FIRST AND CHIEF GROUNDS OF ARCHITECTURE*, 1563, VIII.

had such a system, and as a result, has enjoyed widespread use for centuries. Buildings designed using this rational system, as a general body of work, are of enduring beauty. This is due in part to the fact that such principles are an invaluable aid to those designers of lesser talent. In his *Architecture of Humanism*, Geoffrey Scott reminds the reader that the architects of the past such as Vitruvius, Serlio, Palladio, Vignola, and others, "provided a canon of forms by which even the uninspired architect could secure at least a measure of distinction; and genius, where it existed, could be trusted to use this scholastic learning as a means and not an end."[30]

Ancient Sources

Of the works that have survived, the earliest written record of the rational theory underlying ancient architecture is found in the work of the Roman architect Marcus Vitruvius. Written in the 1st century B.C., his *Ten Books on Architecture* summarizes the mathematical and geometric principles used by the architects of his time. He emphasizes the need for such a system when he says that architecture depends on order as "Order gives due measure to the members of a work considered separately".[31] Vitruvius records for posterity the oral traditions regarding the origins of Western architectural theory. He states that ancient architects studied Nature to discover the inherent proportions found therein. He goes on to describe how the earliest classical columns relied upon the proportional relationship between the average human height in relation to the length of the human foot. Thus, he says, "wishing to set up columns in the temple, but not having rules for their proportion, and being in search of some way by which they could render them fit to bear the load and also of a satisfactory beauty of appearance, they measured the imprint of a man's foot and compared it to his height. On finding that, in a man, the foot was one sixth of his height, they applied the same principle to the column, and reared the shaft, including the capital, to a height six times its thickness at the base. Thus, the Doric column began to exhibit the proportions, strength and beauty of the body of man"[32] (figure 48).

Over time, architects adjusted and experimented with this proportion, developing other visually pleasing ones that evolved into new orders. From the Doric was developed the Ionic, a more slender, delicate order for use in the temple of Diana. This column was one-eighth of its height, more characteristic of the slenderness of women. Furthermore, we learn from Vitruvius that the simple plain shaft of the column was embellished with fluting, or vertical concave grooves, in imitation of "folds in the robes worn by matrons." The Ionic order features two volutes "hanging down on the sides (of the capital) like curly ringlets" completing the feminine allusion (figure 49). Each order in turn had its own mathematically derived system of proportions and ornamentation. As classicism evolved, the proportions for these orders grew thinner and more refined. Ornamentation was created to adorn the orders and delight the eye. Thus, classical architecture showed itself to be a living art form, evolving and refining itself over time.

The climax of this evolutionary development of ancient classicism came in the form of the Corinthian order (figure 50). It was the most elaborate and elegant of the orders and was reserved for use in temples or imperial palaces. Whether or not the story of the origin of the Corinthian capital is based on fact or fancy, the story illustrates how something as artistically exquisite as the Corinthian capital might have had its origin in something as mundane as a wicker basket and an acanthus plant. Morris H. Morgan translates the story from *The Ten Books on Architecture* thus: "A freeborn maiden of Corinth, just of marriageable age, was attacked by an illness and passed away. After her burial, her nurse collected a few little things which used to give the girl pleasure while she was alive and placed them in a basket, carried it to the tomb and laid it on top thereof, covering it with a roof tile so that the things might last longer in the open air. This basket happened to be placed just above the root of an acanthus. The acanthus root, pressed down meanwhile though it was by the weight, when the spring time came around, put forth leaves and stalks in the middle, and

Figure 50. Corinthian Order after Scamozzi, first published in Normand, 1819, Plate 46, reprinted from *Parallel of the Classical Orders of Architecture* (Institute of Classical Architecture & Classical America, Ancanthus Press, 1998).

Figure 51. Origin of the Corinthian Capital. William Chambers, *A Treatise on Civil Architecture* (London, 1759).

the stalks, growing up along the sides of the basket, and pressed out by the corners of the tile through the compulsion of its weight, were forced to bend into volutes at the outer edges (figure 51). Just then, Callimachus, an artist of renown in Athens, passed by the tomb and observed the basket with the tender young leaves growing around it. Delighted with the novel style and form, he built some columns after the pattern for the Corinthians, determined their symmetrical proportions, and established from that time forth the rules to be followed in finished works of the Corinthian order."[33]

It was Vitruvius who first set forth principles by which the perfection of a building might be judged. His three principles are the virtues of *firmitas* (strength), *utilitas* (usefulness), and *venustas* (beauty).[34] By *firmitas*, Vitruvius is referring to the quality and permanence of the building materials used in construction. These materials range from humble wood and brick to the more noble materials of marble, limestone, and granite. *Utilitas* refers to the functional usefulness of a building in meeting its intended use. Thus, Vitruvius is the first to suggest the core idea of the now famous dictum "form follows function." Lastly, Vitruvius includes *venustas*, or beauty, which is of great importance because a building's visual interest often determines its longevity. Recall to your mind buildings that became functionally obsolete but were saved from demolition simply because they were a delight to the eye. Experience shows us that buildings of beauty do indeed have a greater rate of survival than those that are not. Buildings that meet all three criteria often have life spans of centuries, if not millennia.

Vitruvius' concepts of strength, utility, and beauty are foundational elements for architecture of excellence. These have proven themselves to have a tripartite dependency upon one another for the total success of a building. One cannot be ignored simply because of the fulfillment of the other two. An example of such a fallacy would be the proposition that the perfection of a building's utility, or function, will necessarily fulfill its aesthetic requirements. Or similarly, that a building of great aesthetic value will necessarily meet its functional requirements. Each of the three must be considered as a complementary whole.

Proportional Guidelines

Architecture of excellence is characterized by generally defined guidelines for proportion and scale. When matters of proportion and scale are left entirely to the talent and discretion of the architect, buildings of merit may sometimes be the result. However, in many other examples, architecture of mediocrity occurs. There are numerous towns in America and beyond where such guidelines are used successfully to promote architectural designs within a defined vernacular. These include the Village of New Albany, Ohio, and the Florida communities of Seaside, Rosemary Beach, Watercolor, Windsor, and Alys Beach (figures 52–55). These design guidelines address not only the massing of the buildings and the proportions of the windows and doors, but also roof pitch and colors and materials. In England, the town of Poundbury has implemented similar guidelines concerning massing, scale, and materials (figure 56). As a result, these towns have achieved an aesthetic charm that often escapes other communities of similar size and type. In each case, these communities have maintained a consistency of proportion and scale while allowing for a diversity of designs within a defined vernacular. These communities serve to remind us that such guidelines can be a valuable tool in the quest for excellence in our work today.

Architecture devoid of proportional guidelines is an exception and not the rule. The Italian architect Jacopo Borozzi, known as Il Vignola (1507–1573), wrote one of the most enduring treatises on the subject. His book, *Regola delli cinque ordini d'architettura*, is perhaps the most widely studied book on the subject and was reprinted well into the 20th century. In his work, Vignola approaches the subject of architectural proportions from a practical point of view by establishing some basic principles. These principles relate to the design of the classical orders and proved useful to design professionals in a number of cultures. He established these in the form of simple ratios. One example is that the height of the entablature is one-fourth the

FIGURE 52. CHAPEL, SEASIDE, FLORIDA.

Figure 53. Rosemary Beach Town Hall, Rosemary Beach, Florida.

Figure 54. Windsor Town Center, Windsor, Florida.

Figure 55. Proposed building for Alys Beach, Florida.

Figure 56. Poundbury, England.

height of the column, while the pedestal base is one-third the height of the column. This produces an overall ratio of 4:12:3 (figure 57). When there is no base, he simplifies the ratio to 12:3. Vignola makes use of the concept of the *module*, which is the lower diameter of the column shaft. Using the module as a standard unit of measure, he is able to establish rules for a column's height from the bottom of the plinth to the top of the capital. Thus, the Tuscan order has a ratio of 1:7 meaning the column's height is seven times the lower diameter of the column's shaft. Furthermore, he describes the ratio for the Doric order as 1:8, the Ionic as 1:9, and that for the Corinthian and Composite orders as 1:10. These rules of thumb proved to be invaluable for the design and building trades and made mastering the proportions of the classical orders within the grasp of any tradesman. As a result of this approach to the orders, neo-classical buildings often exhibit a continuity and grace that transcends the centuries.

Ironically, it was just this sort of mathematical rationalism that received the most criticism in the 20th century. The primary charge was that it stifles the creative development of architecture as an art form. What these critics disregarded was that rational principles are best used as a starting point for the developing architect. For those with talent, they provide a valuable foundation and a meaningful standard by which future work can be developed. For those having little talent or education, such principles at least serve to save their work from embarrassing deficiencies. Such were the advantages provided by the architectural pattern books of the 18th and 19th centuries. These provided a rational approach to classical architecture that allowed builders and designers to achieve a level of success in their neo-classical buildings. The advantage of such pattern books was that anyone, whether highly trained or not, could master the proportions of the classical orders and their related ornamental vocabulary for buildings of various sizes, shapes, and functions. The rational principles described in these pattern books are one reason why buildings from this period, as a body, are typically aesthetically pleasing. Pages from one

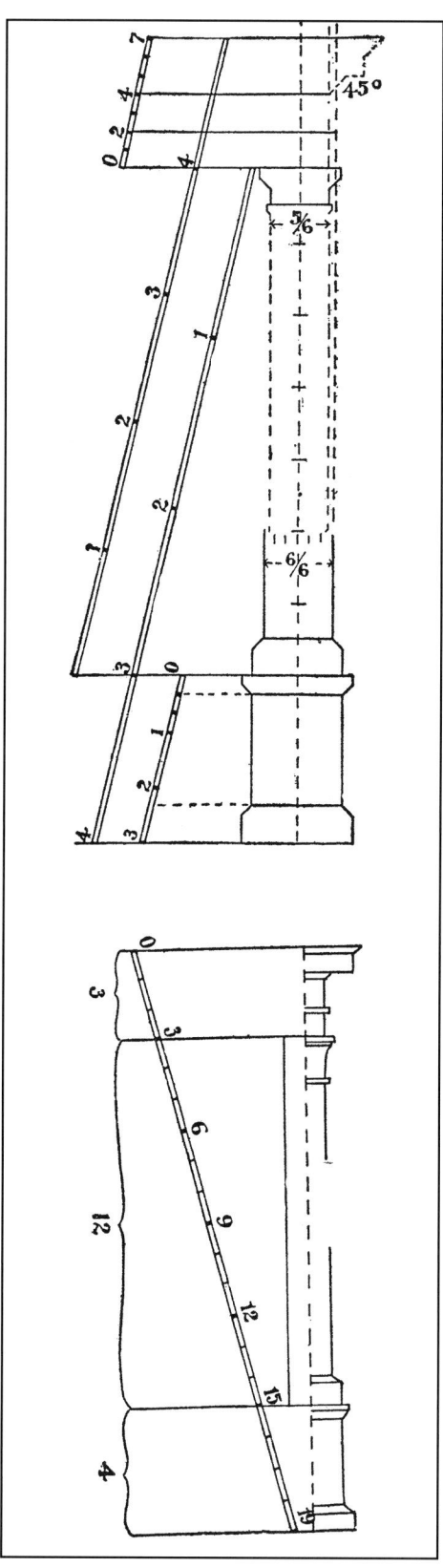

FIGURE 57. PROPORTIONS OF A COLUMN AND ENTABLATURE BY VIGNOLA. WILLIAM R. WARE, *THE AMERICAN VIGNOLA*, SCRANTON INTERNATIONAL TEXT BOOK COMPANY, 1921–22. REPRINT, NORTON LIBRARY, NEW YORK, 1977. P. 32.

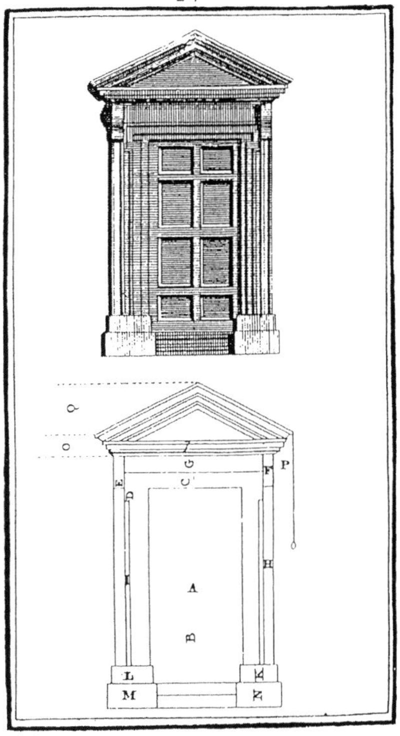

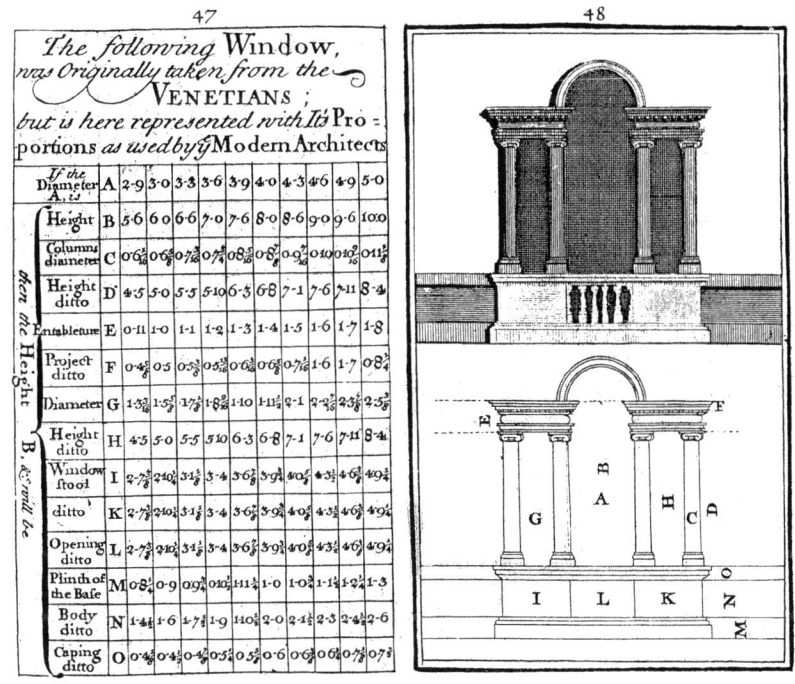

FIGURE 58. RULES OF PROPORTIONS FOR A DOOR AND CASING. WILLIAM HALFPENNY, *PRACTICAL ARCHITECTURE* (LONDON, 1730), PP. 23, 24.

FIGURE 59. RULES OF PROPORTIONS FOR A VENETIAN WINDOW. WILLIAM HALFPENNY, *PRACTICAL ARCHITECTURE* (LONDON, 1730), PP. 47, 48.

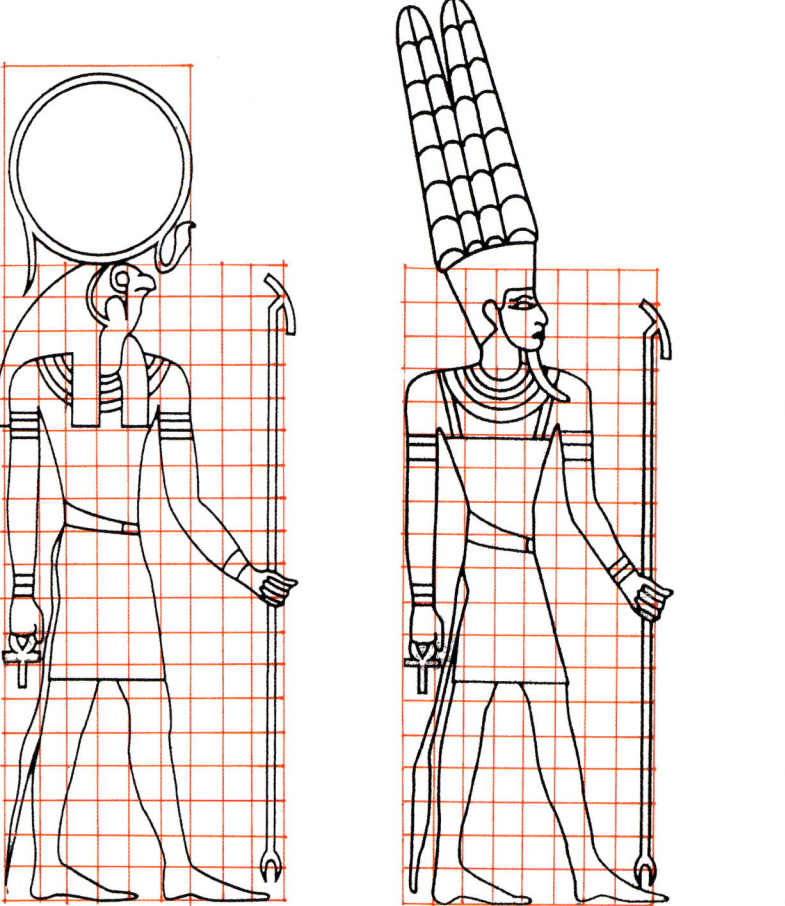

FIGURE 60. EGYPTIAN STANDING MALE FIGURES. M. SEIDEL AND R. SCHULTZ. *ART AND ARCHITECTURE: EGYPT* (NEW YORK: BARNES & NOBLE, 2005).

of these pattern books describing the layouts for a door, its casing and pediment, and that of a Venetian window are illustrated in figures 58–59. In an age before architecture became a formal profession, client and builder alike would consult such works in the formulation of the building's plan and architectural design.

Rationalism in Other Cultures

Civilizations beyond Western Europe have also employed rational principles in their designs. The art of Egypt is known for an amazing uniformity of style over a period of thousands of years. Research by Gay Robins published in *Proportion and Style in Ancient Egypt*, reveals that the basis for this uniformity is the use of a proportional grid system. Walls were prepared for painting by the application of a thin layer of plaster upon which a grid of square lines was created using strings dipped in red paint. The strings were stretched taut across the wall at the desired intervals and then snapped to leave a thin line. Even though the resulting grids were not always perfectly uniform or level, they effectively guided the artist in the task of creating classic forms of Egyptian art. At first, the Egyptian grid system consisted of a vertical line subdivided into six horizontal zones corresponding to anatomical features. Over time, this evolved into a more complex grid 19 units high head to foot and six units wide shoulder to shoulder for a standing male figure

 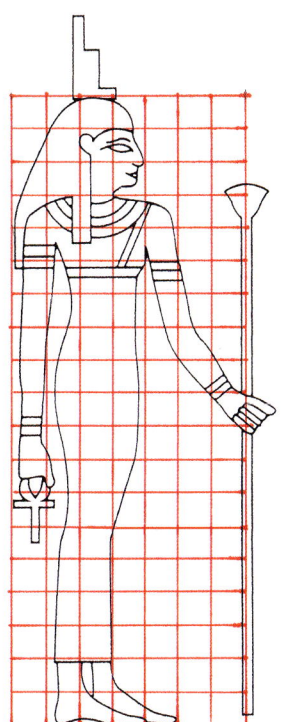

Figure 61. Egyptian standing female figures. M. Seidel and R. Schultz, *Art and Architecture: Egypt* (New York: Barnes & Noble, 2005).

and five units wide for those of females (figures 60–61). For thousands of years, the proportions established for limbs, torso, and facial features were to remain essentially inviolable, with only occasional variations. This accounts for the classic art form that has become emblematic of the Egyptian culture. Grid systems have also been discovered in the art of Minoan Crete and of the Aegean peoples. Investigations may yet reveal to what extent Egyptian architecture is also based upon a proportional grid system.

Islamic architecture and art has been shown to make use of geometric grids as well. Various studies have shown that geometrically complex Islamic art is based on a square plan that is then subdivided into a more complex pattern of interlocking shapes usually in the form of stars (figure 62). These star patterns were perfected between the 12th and 16th centuries and were applied as surface ornament typically in the form of colorful glazed tiles. These patterns are amazingly complex, and until recently little was known about the means by which ancient artisans constructed them. Peter Lu of Harvard University and Peter Steinhardt of Princeton University have studied these star patterns to better understand the secrets of their design. Their research, published in the February 2007 issue of *Science*, theorizes that these patterns are likely the product of pre-made templates of five-pointed and ten-pointed stars. These could be

 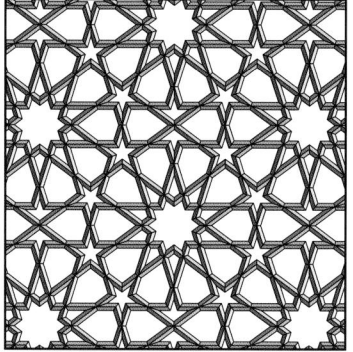 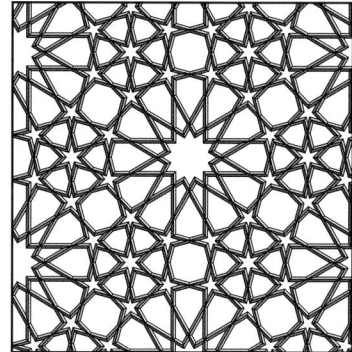

Figure 62. Modern Islamic star patterns. Courtesy of Craig S. Kaplan.

arranged like pieces of a puzzle allowing artisans to create an infinite variety of patterns. Another researcher, Craig S. Kaplan, of the University of Waterloo, is also unlocking the mystery of these star patterns. Using computer-aided models, he has been able to construct similar complex patterns. Through this research, we can gain new respect for the architects and artists who created these intriguing and beautiful works of art.

This sort of rational system produces uniformity and symmetry, both of which are chief characteristics of Islamic art and architecture. This symmetry can be seen throughout the buildings of the Indian sub-continent and the Middle East in the use of repeating uniform parts or geometric patterns. The plan of the Taj Mahal suggests the use of systematic grid systems in the coordination of the layout of both the grounds and the mausoleum. The ground plan by Begley (figure 63) proposes an overlaying grid for the plan and elevations and indicates that the "overall proportions of the complex and the specific locations of certain structures within it appear to have been determined by drawing diagonals across the plan at intervals, usually across every square of 100 yards on a side."[35] As a result of this rational system, Islamic architecture was able to communicate its logical and complex geometry to generations of architects and perfect itself as one of the world's great architectural movements.

The Alhambra, Spain

The Alhambra, or "the red one", is one of the finest and best-preserved Arabian palaces in the world (figure 64). It was begun by Yusuf I and completed by his son Mohammed V in the later half of the 14th century. The exterior of the palace has the appearance of a fortress with its plain thick masonry walls and 22 watchtowers. The austere façade gives no hint of the elaborate and colorful interiors ornamented with glazed tiles, carved woodwork, gold leaf and lapis lazuli. This dramatic contrast symbolizes the Islamic concept that the true riches of life revolve around the inner sanctum of family and spirituality rather than a superficial public show of grandeur. The abundant colorful glazed tiles found throughout the palace have symbolic meaning in addition to their aesthetic appeal. Gold is associated with royalty, red with power, green with paradise, and blue with the hope of attaining paradise. In addition, the walls and architectural details incorporate epigraphs from the Koran in the form of highly stylized calligraphy creating an effect that is both decorative and inspirational.

Almost every surface within the palace is decorated with some geometric pattern or carving. Human or animal forms are generally absent because Islamic tradition, or Hadith, discourages the use of these representations. As a result, Islamic art and architecture developed elaborate floral motifs and decorative geometric

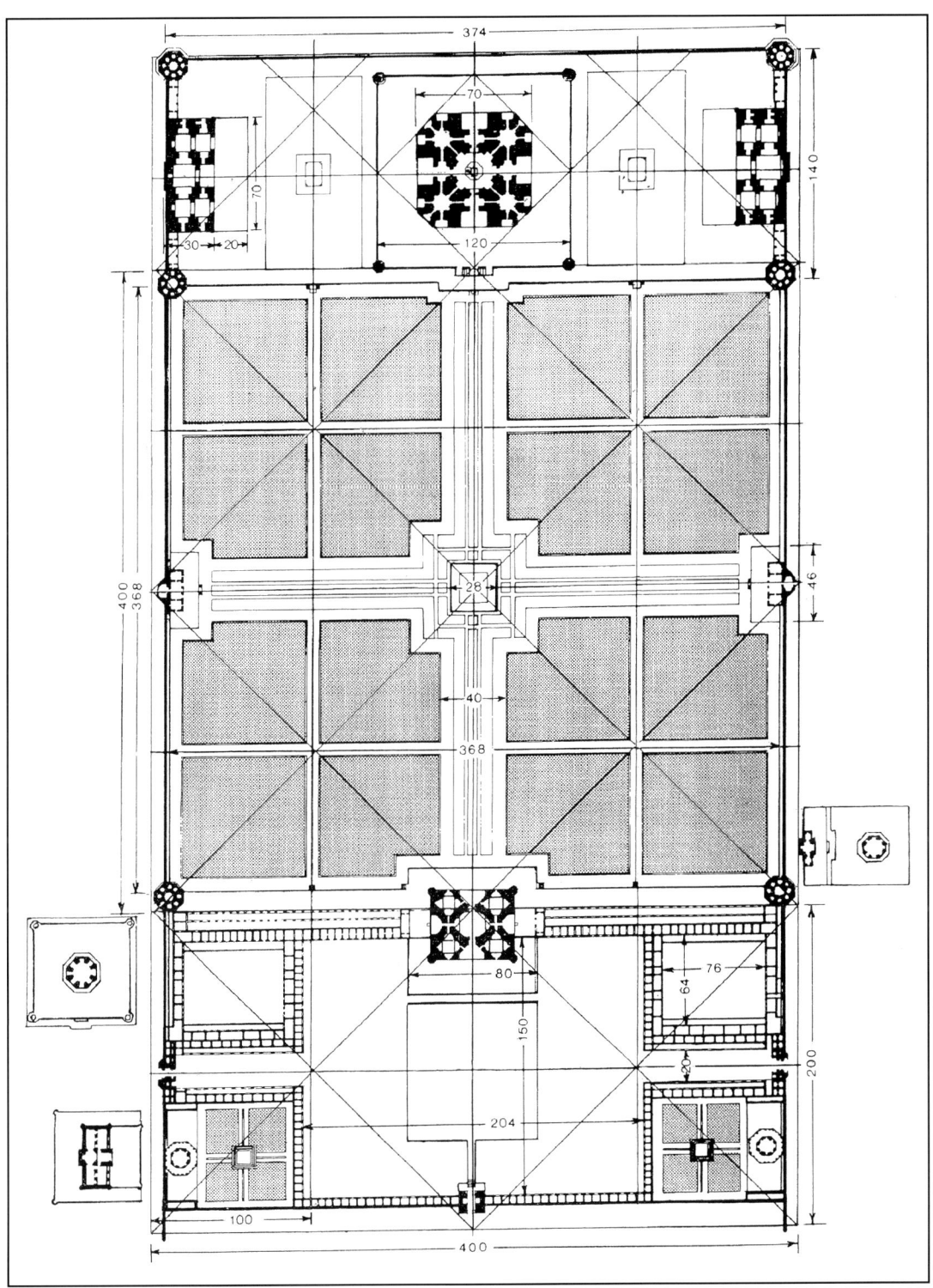

Figure 63. Reconstructed grid plan of the Taj Mahal complex, based on Mughal measurements, W.E. Begley. *Taj Mahal* (Aga Kahn Program for Islamic architecture, University of Washington Press, 1989).

Figure 64. The Alhambra, Granada, Spain.

Figure 65. Window, Alhambra.

patterns based on the square and multi-pointed stars. These elements include the distinctive arches, stucco "stalactites", and geometric filigree window grills (figure 65). These forms are found throughout the Alhambra and have rational geometric relationships underlying their design. In addition to these decorative patterns, the plan of the Alhambra makes use of cube-shaped rooms. In Islamic religious thought, the cube was considered to be the shape of perfection. It is appropriate then that the throne room is a perfect cube representing the wisdom of the monarch. Completing the symbolism of the throne room is the domed ceiling composed of 8,000 inlaid pieces of cedar from Lebanon symbolizing the complexities of the created universe (figure 66). Thus, the Alhambra demonstrates the many ways in which rationalism can be fundamental to the design and ornamentation of an architectural masterpiece.

Figure 66. Throne room ceiling, Alhambra.

CHAPTER 5
NATURE AS THE BASIS FOR EXCELLENCE

When considering a building, we invariably form an opinion as to its aesthetic success. So why is it that certain buildings are more pleasing than others? Are there fundamental principles affecting a building's aesthetic success? Or is beauty, as suggested by Kant, not a function of the object's form but instead based entirely on the mental state of the observer? This brings us to the question at hand—are there natural ratios and rhythms underlying inherent beauty? Architects and artists have studied this question for centuries.

Architecture of excellence is in harmony with Nature. By studying the proportional ratios and rhythms found in Nature, we can learn valuable clues to help our buildings and cities be sympathetic to the natural order of things. As our societies grow larger and more complex, the issue of harmony is relevant to the creation of enduring places in which to live. Such architecture seeks to be a continuum of the created world in scale, proportion, rhythm, and sometimes in its symmetry. The artist Alphonse Mucha (1860–1939) said, "There are certain proportions which serve as principles according to which all organic nature appears to be built up. The loving eye of Nature and of her forms has accustomed itself to these proportions in such a way that it loves to find them elsewhere, particularly in the creations of art."[36] Scale, proportion, rhythm and symmetry are closely related and have to do with different aspects of design. Each is critical to the success of a work of architecture or art. While some persons may be attuned to them at an early age, others can come to master them as an acquired skill developed over time.

Scale

Scale refers to the relative size of something as it relates to objects of its kind or to the human figure. A building is said to be "out of scale" when it is too large or too small in relation

FIGURE 67. ILLUSTRATION COMPARING THE SCALE OF A COTTAGE, A HOUSE AND A PALACE. BUILDINGS FROM ROBERT ADAM, *CLASSICAL ARCHITECTURE* (NEW YORK: ABRAMS, 1990).

to the other buildings surrounding it. Cities adopt laws governing the height and volume of structures that may be built on tracts of land in order to control the scale of buildings. In some cities, building heights are restricted to the width of the street. Arthur Comey, an early pioneer in urban planning said, "The limitation of the height of buildings is an important issue in civic development, for it affects land values, the character of improvements, and the entire outward appearance of the central districts."[37] In addition to buildings, scale is relevant to the design of places such as city centers. It is human-scaled buildings and streets that create harmony between people and their environment. Scale is often the secret why some cities and towns are more well-loved than others. As cities grow larger and more complex, scale is an evermore important factor in their success as places to live. In residences, it is scale that defines whether the structure is considered to be a cottage, a house, or palace (figure 67). Likewise, it is the scale of a piece of land in relation to others around it that determines whether it is classified as an estate parcel. In contrast to these examples, there are some things that remain virtually the same size regardless of the scale of a structure. These items derive their scale from the human figure and include doorknobs, staircases, and the like. Scale is an important component of excellence in design because through it, buildings show themselves to be good neighbors by respecting the surrounding neighborhood. It is proper scale that gives architecture its good manners.

Proportion

In any building or composition there is a relationship or ratio of one part to another and of each part to the whole in regard to height, width, length, and depth. This relationship of volume, between one part and another within a composition, is the meaning of proportion. For example, a person is considered short, tall, thick, or thin in comparison with an established norm for the human figure. A hallmark of great architecture is its concern with the proportional relationships of a building's parts. Alberti expresses this thought most clearly when he says, "As the members of the body are correspondent to each other, so it is fit that one part should answer to another in a building; whence we say that great edifices require great members."[38]

There are two schools of thought on the matter of proportion in architecture. The first takes the position that proportion is normative, like geometry, sometimes using the human body as its basis. In ancient times, it was believed that the ideal proportion for the human figure was considered to be a height six times the length of the human foot.[39] In this manner, it is said, ancient architects first proportioned their columns according to the principle that the height of the shaft was six times the width of the lower part of the shaft, resulting in a ratio of 1:6. These same ancient artisans also constructed sophisticated square root rectangles, which, by coincidence, correspond to the ratios of irrational numbers. This amazing feat could be accomplished by a laborer simply using a square and a string held between two hands. The series of rectangles created in this way begins with a square and progresses with each additional diagonal thereof.

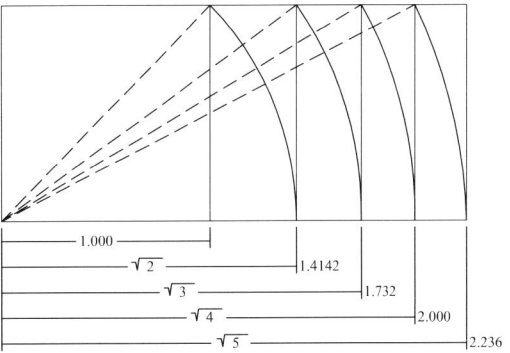

FIGURE 68. RECTANGLES DERIVED BY DIAGONALS.

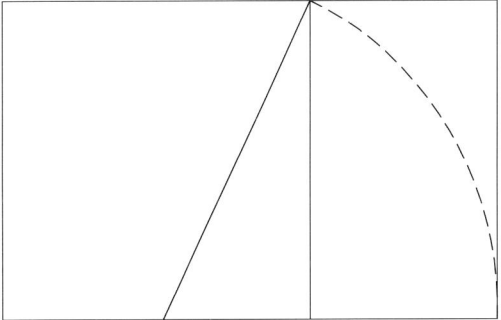

FIGURE 69. GOLDEN MEAN RECTANGLE.

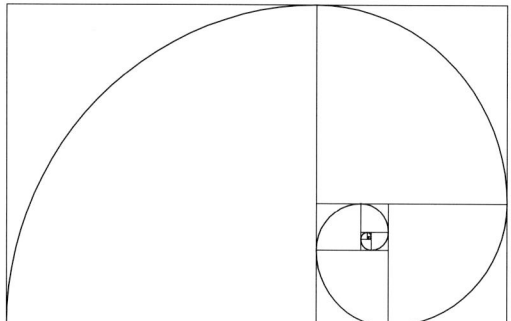

Figure 70. Logarithmic spiral based on Golden Mean rectangle.

The resulting rectangles correspond perfectly with the square root of a small integer (figure 68). Another remarkable achievement was the construction of a Golden Mean rectangle corresponding to the ratio 1:1.618. This shape is derived from the diagonal of a square beginning at the mid-point of one side (figure 69). Golden rectangles can also be constructed using additive squares. As the additive squares are continued, the resulting rectangle approximates more closely the Golden Mean ratio of 1:1.618. Furthermore, a logarithmic spiral is created when a curving line is drawn through diagonally opposite corners of these successive additive squares (figure 70). Of note is the fact that no matter how different in size the line segments may appear, they are not different in shape. This spiral is the most beautiful of mathematical curves and can be found in Greek Ionic capitals and throughout Nature—most famously in the cross section of the nautilus shell.

The Greeks mastered the use of these shapes by incorporating them into their architecture and art. The result is a perfection of proportion that is one factor contributing to their artistic greatness. The Greek philosopher Pythagoras expressed the viewpoint of the time that beauty was associated with these special rectangles. In the 20th century, the Italian architect Giuseppe Terragni (1904–1943) also held this opinion saying, "When that harmony of proportion which induces a state of contemplation, or of a profound feeling in the soul of the observer is joined to the constructive scheme, only then will the crowning result be (a great) work of architecture."[40]

The second thesis is that proportion is arbitrary and is determined by the good taste of the architect as well as by custom and usage. There are many examples of buildings supporting this premise as well. The architecture of the Gothic period does not relate at all to earlier models of classical proportion and yet the resulting architecture is a thing of beauty. Not only does Gothic architecture establish new norms for proportion, it also developed a new order, and a new ornamental vocabulary, which had little basis on the ornament of its Greek and Roman past. In this sense then, one can argue that proportion can be arbitrary and a product of the architect's good taste. However, it is only through continued use and perfection over time that such a proportional system can be validated as having an enduring quality about it.

Rhythm
Rhythm refers to the regular repetition of a form. In architecture, these forms consist of either a series of voids or solid elements such as a series of window or door openings, a row of columns, a series of arches, offsets in the surface of a wall, or some other related sequence (figure 71). The interval of spacing between the forms is usually uniform. However, rhythm can be enriched by combining tighter sequences with broader ones (figure 72), by introducing dissimilar forms between similar forms (figure 73), or by alternating one group of forms with that of another (figure 74).

The organization of rhythms within a building composition often corresponds to a number sequence found throughout Nature developed by the Italian mathematician Leonardo Fibonacci (1170–1250). Fibonacci published a treatise on the advantages of the Arabic system of numeration over that of the Latin titled *Liber Abacis* (1202). It became the standard work on the subject and introduced the use of decimals. The superiority of the Arabic system was immediately apparent, as it is easier to write 88 than the Latin LXXXVIII. *Liber Abacis* also describes the number sequence derived when each successive number is the sum of the previous two numbers such as 0, 1, 2, 3, 5, 8, 13, 21, 34, 55 ... The numbers in this

Figure 71. Simple repetition of forms.

Figure 72. Tighter sequences combined with broader ones.

Figure 73. Dissimilar forms alternating with similar forms.

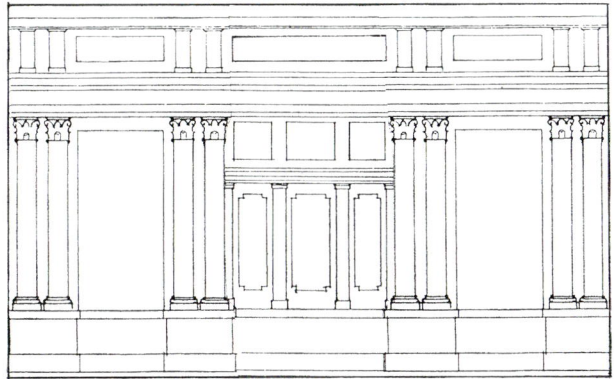
Figure 74. Alternation of one group of forms with that of another.
Figures 71–74 from William R. Ware, *American Vignola* (Norton Library, 1977).

series are prevalent throughout Nature and are found in the design and patterns of plants, the human body, and minerals. In the human body for example (figure 75), we find two hands with five fingers having two or three parts separated by one or two knuckles.

The Fibonacci sequence, as it is called, can be a valuable tool for establishing a building's rhythm. The aesthetic result will be pleasing if the spacing of the openings, arches, or other features is in the series of 1, 2, 3, 5, 8, etc. We find Fibonacci number sequences reflected in buildings from diverse cultures. Many of the best buildings from the past 2,000 years make use of rhythms sympathetic to the Fibonacci number sequence. The following examples incorporate Fibonacci sequences in many ways (figures 76–78).

The Fibonacci sequence is also the basis for a ratio known as the "Golden Mean." The Golden Mean is the ratio 1:1.6 and is derived by dividing

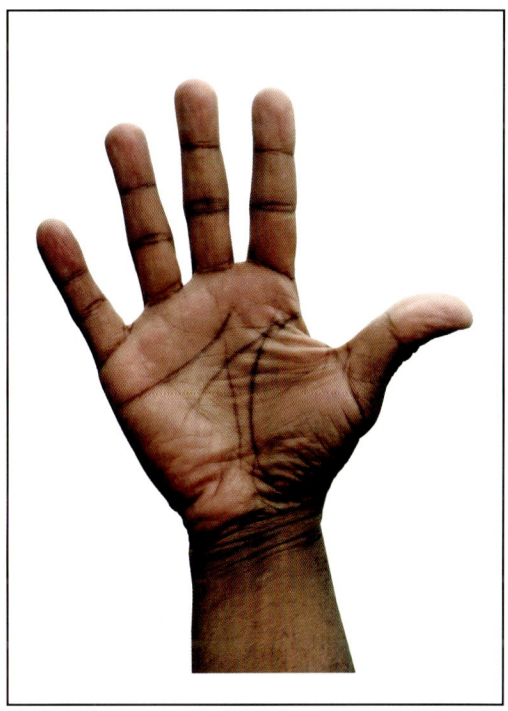
Figure 75. Fibonacci sequence in the human hand—composed of five fingers having two or three parts separated by one or two knuckles.

Figure 76. The Treasury, Petra, Jordan.

Figure 77. Kremlin Cathedral, Moscow, Russia.

Figure 78. Mosque of Mohammad Ali, Cairo, Egypt.

Fibonacci numbers by the previous number. (8/5 = 1.6; 13/8 = 1.6; 21/13 = 1.6; 34/21 = 1.6) Experiment for yourself. Choose two numbers and add them together, then divide the sum by the previous number. The ratio always converges toward 1:1.6. Of even greater interest is the fact that the Golden Mean appears to be the underlying proportional ratio in the design and composition of many plants and animals found throughout Nature. Thus, the Fibonacci number sequence is relevant to both proportion and rhythm.

Symmetry

One of the unifying themes of much of the world's architecture is symmetry. Symmetry is the balance of corresponding parts arranged on either side of a central axis. In D'Aviler's *Dictionnaire* of 1693, symmetry is defined as "the equal correspondence in the parts of a building, either in height, or in breadth, or in length, in order to form a beautiful whole, and Simmetrie Respective is that in which the opposite sides match one another."[41] Because symmetry is found throughout Nature, and especially in the human body, it was believed to be a sacred principle by Renaissance architects. One of these, Leon Battista Alberti said, "It is so agreeable to Nature that the members on the right side should exactly answer the left."[42] Symmetry was the dominant characteristic of the world's monumental architecture until the 19th century. After that time, architects began to experiment with asymmetrical forms, and today these are as common as those that are symmetrical. It is also possible for a work to have variation among its parts on either side of the central axis and still be considered symmetrical, so long as there is a strong correspondence and balance between those parts.

Tidewater, Virginia

The architects of Colonial America used many of these rational principles in the design of their buildings. Much of the architecture of the Tidewater area of Virginia demonstrates these 18th-century architects' appreciation for geometry and symmetry. A typical house of the period (figures 79–80) sometimes had a main body consisting of a double cube, as in this example, or a rectangle having the proportion of the Golden Mean. Furthermore, these architects often used simple radii to determine the proper height for the ridge of the roof and the height of the chimneys. The openings on the façade are arranged in a Fibonacci sequence of five. Other examples from the era would illustrate similar relationships. Architects from this period successfully used rhythms from the Fibonacci number sequence and proportions from the Golden Mean in the design of their buildings. These buildings are sensitive to the principles found in Nature, and this is one reason why they have aged gracefully and have become the cherished architectural treasures of their communities.

Figure 79. The Wythe House, Williamsburg, Virginia.

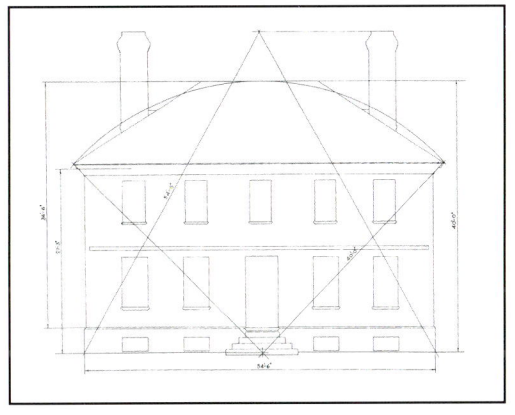

Figure 80. Illustration of geometry of The Wythe House. Marcus Whiffen, *The 18th-Century Houses of Williamsburg* (Historic Williamsburg Foundation, 1960), p. 58.

Figure 81. Petit Trianon, Park of Versailles, France.

The Petit Trianon

One of the most successful buildings to incorporate all of the above principles is the Petit Trianon located on the grounds of Versailles. Originally commissioned by Louis XV and designed by the architect Gabriel in 1761, the Petit Trianon (figure 81) demonstrates Gabriel's virtuosity in the use of cubes and double cubes. This delightful experiment with idealized shapes was meant to create a pavilion of perfect peace and repose since it was believed these proportions would confer such attributes on spaces and forms. Whether or not one agrees with this premise, the resulting building is one of the most beautiful of the 18th century and is considered to be a perfect expression of French neo-classicism. An analysis of the façade shows Gabriel's use of these simple proportions (figure 82). Furthermore, Gabriel employs Corinthian pilasters above a rusticated base to effectively subdivide the façade as he carefully sized and placed the windows and door openings to maintain adherence to the controlling ratios. The building is in perfect scale and harmony with the surrounding park, and each of its façades, though slightly different from one another, is a study in elegant symmetry.

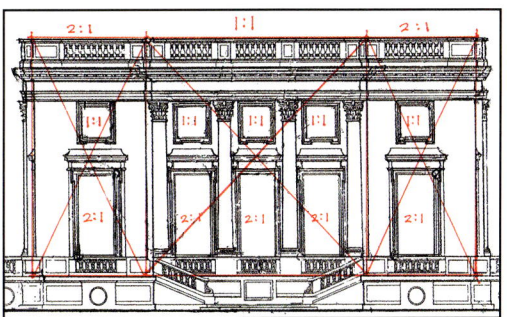

Figure 82. Diagram of the Petit Trianon.

Scientific Studies of Nature

The human figure has been linked to the various theories regarding scale, proportion, rhythm, and symmetry since the time of Vitruvius. Philosophers regarded the human figure to be a divine model from which to draw inspiration, and Renaissance architects in particular studied the human figure for clues regarding these matters. Centuries of buildings were designed according to theories based on this tenet, and it was not until the 20th century that the usefulness of the human figure was challenged along with many of these theories. Recently, however, Joel Primack and Nancy Abrams of the University of California at Santa Cruz have discovered that "the physical size of human beings is roughly midway on the logarithmic scale between the so-called Planck length—the smallest meaningful increment of distance, about 10^{-33} centimeters, and the distance to the edge of the visible universe, the largest meaningful distance, about 10^{28} centimeters."[43] Because of their studies, there now exists scientific grounds upon which one can argue that the human form may indeed have some validity as a model upon which to base such theories. Perhaps now the discussion can be reopened to investigate the ways in which the human form is relevant to scale and proportional theories. Planck and Abrams make the profound observation that, "There is no deeper source of meaning for human beings than to experience our own lives as reflecting the nature and origin of the universe."[44] Is it not appropriate then to investigate in what way our work could reflect this mysterious truth of the universe as well?

Another long-held theory that has fallen out of favor is that some building shapes are more pleasing to the eye than others, especially rectangles based on the square-root of two and the Golden Mean. The premise that such proportions create pleasing shapes and spaces was considered to be embarrassingly naïve by later theorists. However, studies of human optics have found that the overlapping spheres of vision of the human eye fall within a horizontal rectangle having the proportions of 1:1.6, thus approximating the Golden Mean (figure 83). The result of these optical studies suggests that there is indeed a scientific explanation why some shapes are more comfortable to the human

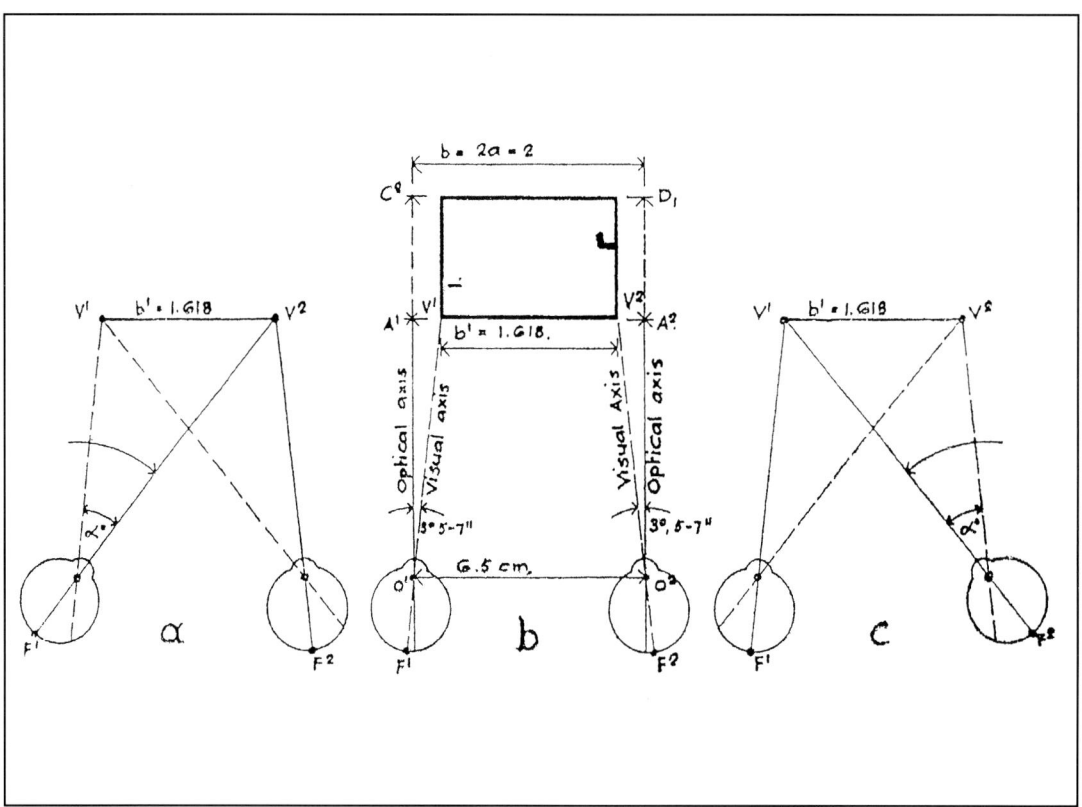

Figure 83. Study of human optics and the Golden Mean.

eye than others. As the human eye becomes accustomed to certain proportions it tends to find those differing from this norm disagreeable. The artist Alphonse Mucha explains this principle, "With great facility, in fact, the eye becomes accustomed to that which it sees most often, and this is also true for the harmonies and finds them agreeable wherever seen; but, on the other hand, when necessary to disturb the customary looks, a fatigue will be felt, and this is translated to the understanding as displeasure."[45] Thus, it may be that the more naturally an object fits within the natural template of the human eye, the more pleasing that object is for us to view. Proportional theories that were once based solely on philosophical and mathematical grounds now have new anthropomorphic data for further study.

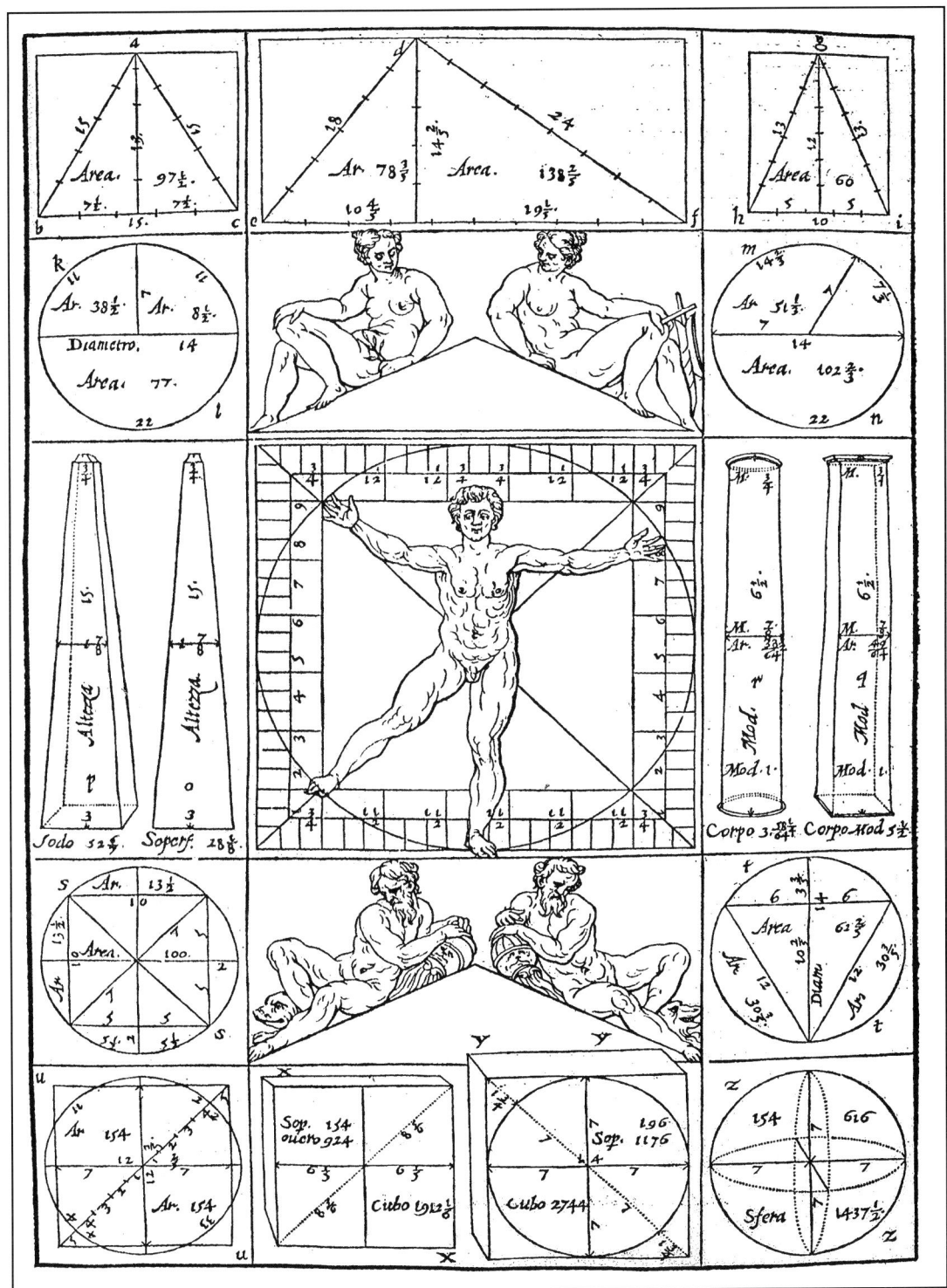

FIGURE 84. ILLUSTRATION OF PROPORTIONS BY SCAMOZZI, *L'IDEA DELLA ARCHITETTURA UNIVERSALE*, VENICE, 1615.

CHAPTER 6
FUNCTION AS THE BASIS FOR DESIGN

The architect Louis I. Kahn once said, "*Form* is what, *design* is how. Form is impersonal, but design belongs to the designer. Design is prescribed by circumstances—how much money there is available, the site, the client, the extent of skill and knowledge, and above all the individual's tendencies of expression. Form is free of conditions. In architecture, it is the realization of a harmony of spaces good for a certain activity of man."[46] Ultimately, it is a building's success in meeting functional needs that defines its true *raison d'etre,* or reason for being. Therefore, architecture of excellence is sympathetic to its function for its expression as a building form.

This was famously expressed in Louis Sullivan's *The Tall Office Building Artistically Considered*, "When native instinct and sensibility shall govern the exercise of our beloved art; when the known law, the respected law, shall be that form ever follows function; then it may be proclaimed that we are on the high-road to a natural and satisfying art, an architecture that will soon become a fine art in the true sense, best sense of the word, an art that will live because it will be of the people, for the people, and by the people."[47] Sullivan's words serve to remind us that no matter how beautiful a building may be, it is ultimately built to serve a purpose and this functional need is the underlying basis for its form and plan. A house, an office building, a government building, and places of worship all have their specific functional needs. Some forms have proven to be enduring solutions for the functional needs for certain types of buildings, and "a persistence in certain solutions of given problems, with only minimal differences between the various solutions"[48] has been the rule for centuries.

Before the design can begin, the architect must first understand the functional requirements demanded of the building based on the culture, customs, and habits of those who will use the building. Because these societal factors are constantly in flux, functional requirements change over time and a variety of forms evolve. Furthermore, a building's success cannot be judged solely on its physical appearance. A building's ultimate purpose is to create an enclosure of space meant to serve a useful purpose. It is the physical experience of working in it, living in it, or passing through it that is the true test of a building's success. To form an opinion of a building based purely on visual observation without considering how well it meets its functional requirements, is to fall short of a true evaluation of that building.

A building's plan is most successful when it meets its functional requirements while showing itself flexible for changing future needs. Such a building is more likely to be emulated by others and its longevity as a type and form greatly enhanced. Similarly, if a building falls short of meeting its functional requirements in either the short run or the long run, then its survival is entirely dependant upon its aesthetic success. Since society's needs change, most buildings eventually fall short of their functional requirements. When this occurs, a building's inherent beauty is a critical factor in its survival. Buildings of beauty tend to be preserved, remodeled, or adaptively reused. Buildings failing in this respect are usually demolished. It is important to state at this point that beauty in architecture is not the result of a perfect functionalism as some theorists have suggested. Rather, beauty in architecture is the result of the architect's conscious effort to transform functional space into a tangible artistic expression. The more successful an architect is in achieving this goal, the more successful the building. There are numerous examples of this truth.

The Amphitheater

The ideal plan for an amphitheater was worked out by the Greeks and Romans and this form has remained virtually unchanged for thousands of years. The form of amphitheaters evolved over time to include three basic stage forms: the *arena*, in which the stage is encircled by the spectators; the Greek *theater* with its stage projecting into the audience with the spectators arranged in an arc; and the Renaissance open *proscenium*, where stage and spectators are apart.[49] The earliest theaters were little more than a flat area, sometimes paved, with wooden benches for the spectators. These early performances were religious rituals performed in honor of Dionysus with the spectators more like participants in worship. Eventually, the built form was made more permanent with rows of stone seats in a semicircle. By the 4th century B.C., the theater had achieved its classical form as found at the Theater of Epidauros. This theater was designed by Polycleitus the Younger and quickly became known for its excellent acoustics and elegant form. Many other ancient examples have come down to us such as those found in Athens, Delos, Delphi, Sparta, and Caesarea. The Theater of Aspendus (figure 85) exhibits many elements that are quite familiar to us today. The semicircular seating is arranged in concentric rows ascending as if in a truncated cone (figure 86). The area in front of the stage, called the *orchestra*, is usually situated no more than 5 feet below the level of the stage itself. In Roman theaters, the area of the orchestra was reserved as seating for the Senatorial class. The general seating of concentrically rising rows is subdivided by aisles occurring in uniform intervals, and these in turn are intersected by a wide cross-aisle about halfway up the body of the theater. Great care was taken to assure that this cross-aisle was not so wide that it would prevent a line drawn along the top edge of the seats from the lowest to the highest seat from touching. In all cases, these theaters were designed to

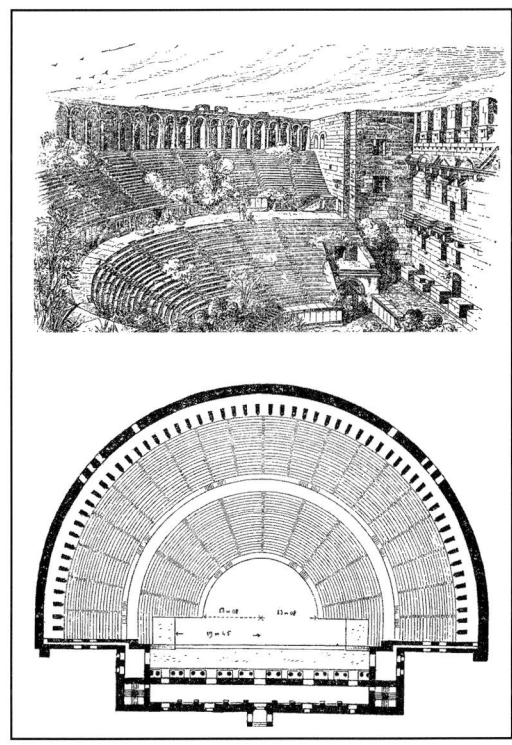

Figure 85. Theater of Aspendus.

Vitruvius, *Ten Books on Architecture*. English translation by Morris Hickey Morgan, (originally published by Harvard University Press, 1914; reprinted in New York: Dover Publications, 1960), Ch. VI. p. 149.

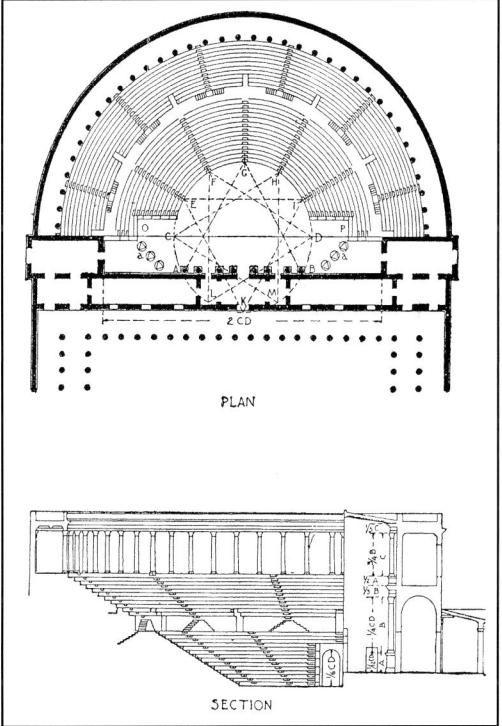

Figure 86. A Roman Theatre According to Vitruvius.

Vitruvius, *Ten Books on Architecture*. English translation by Morris Hickey Morgan, (originally published by Harvard University Press, 1914; reprinted in New York: Dover Publications, 1960), Ch. VI. p.147.

allow for easy access and exit of large crowds. Furthermore, the architects studied harmonics and became skilled in understanding the geometry required for good sound transmission to all listeners. Because the harmonics of such a design was found to be conducive for both dramatic and musical performances, the basic design of theaters has remained essentially along these lines for thousands of years. Even today, we can find similar arrangements in our modern amphitheaters.

Basilicas and Cathedrals
Another building form that has successfully met a functional need for millennia is that of the *basilica* or church. For the first 250 years of its existence, Christianity had no architecture to call its own because early churches met in private homes. Thus there was no established form during this early period. Christianity differed from almost all the other religions of its time because it required no blood sacrifice. Rather, its two primary sacraments—baptism and the Lord's Supper—had no architectural requirements. It was only after the conversion of the Emperor Constantine in the 4th century A.D., and the legalization of Christianity, that a new form of building was required to accommodate the growing number of worshipers. These first sanctuaries, or basilicas, were modeled after Roman law courts in which the judge was seated at the far end of a long hall and all others stood. This is the first distinct Christian architectural form. These first basilicas only provided seats for the Bishop and assisting ministers near the altar while the main hall, or *nave*, had no seating other than low ledges along the sides for the elderly and infirm. The congregation stood throughout the worship service, or Mass.

Early Christian church architecture contrasted sharply with pagan building forms. Pagan temples were built to house an idol and store offerings. Christian churches were built to house the people of the new faith. As such, Christian churches were more concerned with the function of the interior space than with the building's external appearance. This is in marked contrast to the pagan temples that devoted great attention to external architectural beauty. The façades of early churches are often plain with simple sculptural decoration. However, the interiors were richly decorated with marble and colorful mosaics.

The basilica's plan was well suited for the needs of these first congregations. Every aspect of the plan and its architecture was devoted to directing the focus of the congregation toward the east and the altar where the Lord's Supper

FIGURE 87. CHURCH OF SANTA MARIA MAGGIORE, ROME, ITALY.

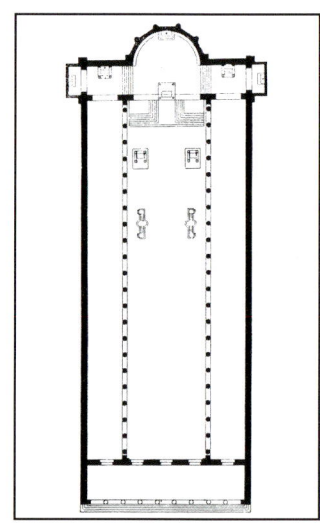

EARLY PLAN OF SANTA MARIA MAGGIORE.

Figure 88. St. Mark's Basilica, Venice, Italy.

was celebrated. People stood or knelt in the nave during Mass and merely moved out of the way when a procession took place. One of the oldest surviving examples of such a basilica is the Church of Santa Maria Maggiore in Rome (figure 87). The basilica's geometric massing consists of a tall central nave with gable roof flanked by shorter side aisles. The church's original plan with its central nave and flanking side aisles dates to 432 A.D. The long central nave is lined with columns of Athenian marble believed to have been reused from an earlier Roman building. The linear rhythm of these columns focuses the worshiper's attention on the central altar. The church's gilded mosaics, the oldest of their type in Rome, illustrate Old Testament stories and inspire the worshipers through their illustration of biblical themes. Santa Maria Maggiore's form inspired countless other basilicas and is still serving the functional needs of its congregation today.

St. Mark's Basilica in Venice is considered to be one of the best examples of Byzantine church architecture (figure 88). Built around 1050, it is modeled on the earlier churches of Hagia Sophia and the Church of the Holy Apostles both located in Constantinople. It is a Greek cross plan having a central dome over the main crossing and four smaller domes over each of its four arms of equal length. It represents a new building form, which allowed a larger number of worshipers to approach the altar during the Mass.

By the Middle Ages the innovative architecture of the Gothic period was infusing Europe with a soaring new architecture and a plan that now included side transepts or cross aisles. These transepts created a building plan in the shape of a cross as found at Chartres Cathedral (figure 89). Furthermore, the plan had evolved to include a chancel area between the nave and the high altar. The chancel is sometimes separated by a screen from the nave, effectively separating the average worshiper from close proximity to the high altar. The chancel had pews on its sides facing inward toward the central aisle. This seating was reserved for clergy and wealthy laity. Multiple smaller chapels were also placed around the

Figure 89. The Cathedral of our Lady of Chartres. Chartres, France. 1194–1220.

sides of the nave so Masses could be performed simultaneously. Seating was still not provided in the nave so that people were required to stand, moving from chapel to chapel as Masses were said. By the 1400s, isolated bench seats were provided to enable worshipers to pray more comfortably.

During the Protestant Reformation of the 1500s, the church's functional requirements evolved further. There was a movement to bring people nearer the altar and a new emphasis on teaching during the worship. For the first time, pews were provided for the whole congregation and sermons were introduced as a regular part of the service. The older church and cathedral plans proved flexible to meet these new requirements and were retrofitted with pews and lecterns for the sermons. Furthermore, chancel screens were sometimes removed and the altar moved forward toward the crossing of the nave and transepts to bring the sacrament of the Lord's Supper closer to the people.

Three hundred years later, church functional requirements evolved again and a central nave plan was developed, as can be seen in the landmark design for Trinity Church in Boston (figure 90). Designed by H.H. Richardson in 1877, this new plan was a radical departure from central nave architecture and ushered in an era of church design that created an inclusive open auditorium. Richardson extended the transepts to form a Greek cross having the chancel, transepts, and nave of equal size grouped around a central square creating a massive openness. Trinity Church is an example of a church plan that more closely resembles the seating arrangement of an auditorium. This novel plan illustrates the cultural shift of worship from the traditional focus on the altar to a more community-focused worship centered on the preaching of the Gospel.

Houses

"Is there anything more pleasurable than a house in which our needs are perfectly satisfied? It brings delight to our lives and helps us to spend our days in happiness."[50] Of all the buildings of mankind, perhaps none is more personal or close to our hearts than the house. It is most likely the first structure erected by man. Houses are the buildings over which we as individuals exert the most control through the personalization of the interior space and sometimes of the exterior as well. Because of the personal and emotional investment in our houses, they become more than just "spaces good to live in"[51] and take on the more immediate concept of "home."

Figure 90. Trinity Church. Boston, Massachusetts.

Houses are a complex building form because they are required to meet a multiplicity of needs. At its fundamental level, a house provides shelter from the elements, a place to nourish the family, and lodging in which to sleep. Beyond these needs, a house's functional requirements can be expanded to include a variety of social and entertainment uses that can transform a simple cottage into a castle. Carried to its extreme, a house can become a huge complex containing not just rooms for habitation but also galleries for the display of art, ballrooms and banquet halls for large entertainments, spaces for worship, and extensive service wings and staff quarters.

As a testament to the ever-changing human condition and the fluidity of cultures, the house as a form is always in flux. Each evolutionary form of the house, as it responds to societal changes, new technologies, and materials, is a telling reflection of its particular time and place. A plan that was once considered the ultimate in luxurious housing can become, in just one or two generations, "unlivable" and thus, obsolete. The villas of the Roman Empire found in the excavations at Pompeii were certainly the ultimate in comfortable living in their day (figure 91). The same could be said of the manor houses of 12th-century French nobility, the city palaces of Renaissance Italian merchants (figure 92), or the elegant châteaux of 16th-century France (figure 93). Yet, all of these, in their original form, would be considered untenable today if not modernized. In many cases, the societal conditions that supported these households no longer exist. Until the 20th century, most grand homes required full-time staff to support them. With the passing of that era, entire wings of these homes have fallen into disuse. Furthermore, family life in some societies is more informal than in previous generations—demanding a more relaxed floor plan arrangement than had previously been the norm. In other cases, the security issues that drove their designs no longer exist and their thick masonry walls and damp moats are now a hindrance rather than an advantage. Ultimately, however, it is advancements in technology that eventually make all residences obsolete. With the

Figure 91. House of Venus, Pompeii, Italy.

Figure 92. Palazzo Vecchio, Florence, Italy, 14th century.

Figure 93. Château de Chenonceau, France, 1522.

invention of indoor plumbing, electricity, central heating and air conditioning, or the wiring required for Internet access or cable television, all houses eventually require updating. Thus, unlike amphitheaters and basilicas, houses have not evolved into an idealized form in the same general kind of way.

While there are those who would distill the house down to little more than a "machine for living", as did Le Corbusier, the best houses do more than just fulfill functional needs. In its best form, a house also provides visual delight to its inhabitants. The great houses of history demonstrate an infinite variety of ways to produce this visual delight through color, form, and texture. Conversely, houses having little aesthetic value are at risk of demolition when they become technologically obsolete because they are not considered to be worth the investment of additional work. The proof of this premise is the body of houses that have come down to us over the centuries, all of which have strong aesthetic considerations.

Tall Buildings

There is perhaps no building form more representational of the 20th century than the tall building commonly known as the skyscraper. This new building type first appeared in Chicago; a product of the city's need for commercial office space after the devastating fire of 1871 and made more acute by the city's already exponential growth. The tall building owes its genesis to new technologies—the elevator and steel frame construction. One of the first architects to experiment with this new building form was Louis Sullivan (1856–1924) in conjunction with his partner Dankmar Adler (1844–1900). It was their work in Chicago that established many of the foundational elements associated with tall building design. One of the best-known buildings by this firm was the Carson, Pirie, Scott Building begun in 1899 (figure 94). As described by Sigfried Gideon, the building "remains unsurpassed in its expressive strength. The interior is still of the warehouse type, with continuous, unbroken floor areas ... Its basic elements are the horizontally elongated "Chicago windows," admirably homogenous and treated to coincide with the framework of the skeleton. The whole front is executed with strength and precision that is matched by no other building of the period."[52] In reflecting on his role in developing this new building type, Adler said, "We are allowed the privilege of participating in the creation and in witnessing the birth of another epoch of architectural design, the form or style of which will be founded upon the discovery of the steel pillar, the steel beam, the clear sheet of glass, electric light and mechanical ventilation, all devoted to the service of functions or wants created by the greater intensity of modern life and by improved means of communication between places and man."[53] Thus, the tall building developed as a result of the new functional requirements of modern business.

Initially, tall building design experimented with building forms clad in stone and brick with horizontal plate glass combined with operable double-hung windows. These early architects were quite inventive in their approach to the new building form within the traditional vernacular of the time. The form of the tall building was determined very early on by its function of providing a higher density of office space within an urban setting. This was no easy task since they did not fit neatly within the context of traditional architecture because of their scale and form. The only prototypes for vertical buildings of this scale were the cathedrals of the Gothic style. So it was not surprising then that Cass Gilbert (1859–1934) drew upon the Gothic for inspiration for

FIGURE 94. CARSON, PIRIE, SCOTT BUILDING, CHICAGO, ILLINOIS.

Figure 95. Woolworth Building, New York City, New York.

the design of the Woolworth Building of 1913 (figure 95). The tallest building in the world when it was completed, the Woolworth Building successfully incorporated Gothic detailing into its architectural form to create a building of elegance and style. The building is seen from all four sides, so each is carefully treated architecturally and incorporates gargoyles, turrets, pinnacles, flying buttresses, and colored terra cotta. It was so successful that it engendered many other tall buildings in a similar style that came to be known as "Woolworth Gothic."

The next turning point for the design of the tall building occurred in 1922 on the occasion of an architectural competition for the design of the Chicago Tribune Building. The stated goal of the competition was to "design the most beautiful office building in the world."[54] Over 260 entries were received from architects from around the world. The designs submitted by the three finalists would have far-reaching influence on the design of the next generation of tall buildings. The winning entry by John Mead Howells (1868–1959) and his partner Raymond M. Hood (1881–1934) was a Neo-Gothic structure (figure 96) reminiscent of Cass Gilbert's Woolworth Building of the previous decade. But it was the second-place entry by Finnish architect Eliel Saarinen (1873–1950) with its Art Deco styling and clean lines that would prove to be more reflective of the next generation of tall building design.

The Art Deco style would find its full expression in the 77-story Chrysler Building of 1930 (figure 97). The architect William van Alen (1883–1954) clad the building in brick, making it the tallest brick building in the world. The building also premiered the use of Nirosta, a nickel–steel alloy, in the cladding of the building's distinctive multi-tiered spire. Van Alen's architecture makes playful reference to the automobile in homage to Chrysler by including ornamental hubcaps, wheels, fenders, and hood ornaments on the building's façade. The Chrysler Building is one of the last great tall buildings to be built before the economic depression of the 1930s put a temporary stop to tall building construction.

When tall buildings began to be built again after the Second World War a decade later, it would be in a totally new style using the next generation of building materials and building techniques.

A major factor in the transition to this new style of tall building design was the opening of the landmark exhibit *Modern Architecture* in New York in 1932. This exhibition brought the "International style" to the public's attention by showcasing the work of Gropius, Mies van der Rohe, Le Corbusier, Wright, Neutra, and others. The exhibit was organized by Philip Johnson and Henry-Russell Hitchcock and sponsored by the Museum of Modern Art in New York City. The basic tenets of the International style were summarized by Johnson and Hitchcock as: 1) an emphasis on volume and space over mass and solidity; 2) an emphasis on regularity instead of symmetry; and 3) an emphasis on exposed materials instead of

Figure 96. The Chicago Tribune Tower, Chicago.

Figure 97. Chrysler Building, New York City, New York.

applied ornament.⁵⁵ These tenets, along with Sullivan's dictum that "form follows function," would set the design of tall buildings on a course toward a pure functionalism resulting in "glass box architecture." Driven by business economics more than aesthetic considerations, International-style tall buildings took on the form of rectangular, flat-roofed structures having repetitive rhythms of glass panels within a grid of steel or concrete. The overriding goal of these buildings was to provide as much commercial space as economically as possible.

One of the foremost architects of International-style tall buildings was Ludwig Mies van der Rohe (1886–1969). Originally the director of the German Bauhaus, Mies immigrated to America in the late 1930s and brought with him the ideals of the International style. In summarizing his philosophy on tall buildings, Mies said, "The office building is a house of work, of organization, of clarity, of economy. Bright, wide workrooms, easy to oversee, undivided except as the undertaking is divided. The maximum effect with the minimum expenditure of means. The materials are concrete, iron, glass."⁵⁶ His most famous building illustrating these points is the Seagram Building (figure 123) in New York City. This building was built in 1958 on Park Avenue and became the inspiration for the next generation of tall buildings throughout the world. His approach of reducing volumes to its simplest form was acclaimed for its so-called "elegant solution" to the problem of creating office space within an urban context. The Seagram Building was one of the first tall buildings utilizing a bronze colored metal skin with bronze tinted glass. Ironically, the non-structural vertical I-beams that Mies placed across the building's façade to provide visual relief to its otherwise flat surface have been criticized by both International School purists who find such superficial ornamentation unnecessary and by traditionalists who object to the I-beams on purely aesthetic grounds. As a type, the Seagram building remains true to the functionalist principles of the International School through its simple geometric massing and avoidance of any traditional references.

During the 1970s, architects began to experiment with traditional details, shapes, and forms in an attempt to provide some relief from the austere geometric functionalism of the previous two decades. Underlying this movement, known as Post-Modernism, was a longing for buildings to once again invoke a known and familiar past. However, Post-Modernism's broad range of elements and materials makes it difficult to describe as a specific style. Some of the early Post-Modern buildings were criticized for their eclectic or superficial use of historical models. The more mature work from this period, however, has resulted in some excellent designs that have inspired other buildings by their form and use of noble materials. One of the most successful of these is 333 Wacker Drive, Chicago, Illinois (figure 98). It was designed by Kohn Pedersen Fox Associates PC in 1983 and

FIGURE 98. 333 WACKER DRIVE, CHICAGO, ILLINOIS. COURTESY OF KOHN, PEDERSEN FOX ASSOCIATES PC.

was widely acclaimed for its massing and design. Its architects began to free themselves from the straight lines and grids of the International School and experimented with curved walls and a mixture of natural materials. The result is a building that still looks fresh several decades after its construction. Another example of a Post-Modern tall building that has shown aesthetic longevity is 191 Peachtree Tower, Atlanta, Georgia (figure 99). Designed by Johnson/Burgee Architects and Kendall/Heaton Associates, the building was completed in 1990. The building's façade is veneered in Rosa Dante granite and features two distinctive roof towers that provide traditional references and details.

Perhaps the biggest challenge facing tall building design today is the reintegration of the principles that will help these buildings engage the culture and stand the test of time. While it is imperative that all buildings meet their functional requirements, meeting functional requirements alone will not guarantee the aesthetic success of a building. In fact, relying entirely on a building's function for its form leads to abuses from which our cities are yet to recover. Furthermore, the trend toward super-tall buildings is challenging our aesthetic sensibilities and our cities in new ways. In addition to the density of people and traffic such buildings generate, super-tall buildings dwarf their neighbors by their scale and challenge the use of materials other than glass and steel. The designers of these buildings have experimented with every twist, turn, and curve possible to lend these enormous towers some artistic distinction as they dominate the skyline of their respective cities.

The larger question to be determined is what is the long-term sustainability of super-tall buildings over a period of hundreds of years? Since all buildings eventually need renovating, what will be their fate just a few generations from now? Will their aesthetics justify the huge cost to refurbish? Will demolition ever be an option due to the cost and logistics associated with buildings of this size? These are the dilemmas that will face the generation that must come to terms with these buildings as they age. The day may come when super-tall buildings will be seen as liabilities, and societies will be more reluctant to build them. Just because a society *can* build such buildings doesn't mean that they *should* build them.

There are, however, tall buildings that have achieved aesthetic success in this most challenging of building forms. One of these is the Petronas Towers in Kuala Lumpur, Malaysia designed by Cesar Pelli & Associates (figure 100). The Petronas Towers were the world's tallest buildings in 1996, rising 452 meters. These buildings form the centerpiece for the new mixed-use district of the Kuala Lumpur City Centre complex. The 88-story towers combine office, retail, and entertainment functions within one complex and provide 218,000 square meters of floor space. In addition to the towers, the complex includes an 880-seat concert hall, an art gallery, a library, an

Figure 99. 191 Peachtree Tower, Atlanta, Georgia.

Figure 100. Petronas Towers, Kuala Lumpur, Malaysia.

interactive science discovery center, a 44-story annex building, and an underground parking garage for 5,400 cars. The towers utilize several innovative construction technologies such as the use of unusually high-strength concrete to facilitate the buildings' soft-tube structural system. The buildings' double-deck elevators transport 26 persons per deck and their energy conservation system, based on "cool-recovery" technology, is estimated to reduce the buildings' energy requirement by half. It is the buildings' reference to Islamic design motifs and its extensive use of local materials, however, that visually sets them apart from other such projects. The buildings' basic plan utilizes interlocking squares to form a traditional Islamic eight-pointed star that is further enlarged with semicircular inserts in the angle of the corners to create more floor space. The buildings' tapered shafts and distinctive finials allude to Malaysian design motifs. The Petronas Towers complex succeeds in combining local traditions and materials with modern technology and construction techniques to create a building complex that has become a popular icon for the region.

An example of another modern building that speaks to the principles of architectural excellence is 15 Central Park West (figure 101). This 201-unit condominium residence building, located in New York City, might even be described as being avant-garde because of its stylistic break with the previous generation of glass-box residential high-rises. Designed by New York-based architect Robert A.M. Stern in association with SLCE Architects, this building achieves a high level of success on all accounts as evidenced by its strong sales record and the positive response it has received from the community at large. The 15 Central Park West building embraces and reinterprets traditional elements rather than rejecting them as passé. These elements include its natural limestone cladding, defined windows, and floor plans that offer separate living and dining rooms as opposed to open plans of undefined space. The building's architecture represents continuity with the city's building traditions through its natural materials, the proportion of its massing, its scale to the surrounding buildings and street, the rhythm of its windows, and the articulation at the top of its tower.

One factor in the building's success is its conscious attempt to offer its residents maximum functionality. Unlike older residential buildings surrounding Central Park, this building provides underground parking for its residents, an off-street arrival court for guests, an in-house chef for private catering, a library, a wine cellar offering individual private climate-controlled storage, a fitness center with a 75-foot lap pool, a screening room for movies, and an in-house business center with conference room. Thus, this building touches on all of the principles of excellence to a degree seldom found in other buildings of its type. Because of this, the developer has been handsomely rewarded and the residents have a building of sublime beauty and functionality that meets the needs of a modern luxury lifestyle.

Figure 101. 15 Central Park West, New York City, New York.

CHAPTER 7
Materials and Design

Building materials have traditionally been classified as being either *noble* or *base*. The noble materials of marble, granite, limestone, and bronze are associated with public buildings or grand residences primarily because of their beauty, durability, rarity, and cost. The base materials of wood, brick, concrete, clay, and fiber are associated with the more common buildings of everyday life such as houses, shops, and factories. The noble materials have proven themselves to possess a high degree of durability over a long period of time. They have strong associations with buildings of quality, while the base materials have varying degrees of durability with some maintenance required to extend their life.

Noble Materials

From earliest times, the most precious and durable materials were reserved for society's most important buildings. The examples that have come down to us from millennia past are almost all religious in nature. The oldest of these are the temples of Egypt, which are constructed of native sandstone. Their massive forms, with elaborate relief carvings, stand today as mute witnesses to their long-past civilization along the Nile. Sandstone is a relatively soft material that is prone to water erosion. However, due to the arid conditions of Egypt, these temples have survived the onslaught of time relatively intact. Other civilizations such as those of the Greeks, made their temples of masonry and these structures have also survived to give us a glimpse of the glory that was once Greece. In most instances, the destruction that has occurred to these buildings has been the result of an earthquake or other natural event. But it is the destruction by man that has often taken the greatest toll. The Parthenon was essentially intact up until 1687 when an artillery shell hit the temple and detonated a store of ammunition inside the building. The resulting explosion left the building in the shattered state that we see it today. If the Parthenon had been made of a base material such as wood or brick, it is doubtful any of the structure would have survived to our time. The Athenians constructed their temple of fine Pentelic marble to honor their deity and in so doing created a building that has survived, albeit shattered, through the ages.

It is a commitment to quality and permanence that best characterizes the choice of noble materials. Their very hardness, variety of color, and rarity set them apart as premium building materials. Marble and granite in particular offer the widest selections of color and graining. These are often used for the adornment of interiors due to their hardness and durability. These colorful stones are used as paving stones for floors, on the walls as decorative panels, and even on the ceilings in the form of mosaic tile. One of the oldest existing structures using noble materials in this way is St. Mark's Basilica in Venice, Italy. Constructed on marshland, the entire building is built over wood pilings driven deep into the soggy soil. It is a miraculous survivor from the 11th century and is in continuous use today. St. Mark's is an interesting example because it makes use of noble building materials that were reused from earlier churches and palaces of Constantinople. Because of this, many of its ornate columns vary in height, color, material, and design. The most rare of these are made of porphyry, a purplish colored stone. Ancient porphyry was mined from an isolated quarry in the Eastern Desert of Egypt. Because of its rarity, it was used to embellish imperial buildings such as the Roman Pantheon and for royal tombs. In addition to porphyry, the walls of St. Mark's are veneered in various marbles and its ceiling tiled in gold and polychrome mosaic depicting biblical imagery (figure 102). Buildings having this sort of varied history over an expanse of millennia are more likely to survive when made of durable materials such as marble, granite, limestone, and bronze.

Base Materials

While the materials of brick and concrete are more common in their use, this in no way means that they cannot make a significant contribution to a society's built environment. Much of ancient Egypt's and Mesopotamia's architecture was built of a brick core and veneered in stone or tile. Because of the impermanent nature of this sun-baked brick, these buildings have not survived the weathering of the centuries. However, one brick building from antiquity that has survived is the Roman Pantheon. In large part, its survival is due to the use of oven-baked brick and the hard lime-based concrete that was used as a mortar. The Romans perfected the use of concrete in their buildings. Unlike some modern buildings, the Romans used concrete as a core material rather than as a primary surface material. Roman concrete and brick were the structural skeleton supporting the more noble materials of marble, granite, limestone, and bronze.

Wood has proven itself to be the most flexible of all the building materials as well as being the most widely used among the nations of the world. It has been theorized that the first structures erected by man were wood frames combined with fiber mats. While none of these early structures have survived, clay models of such buildings have come down to us giving evidence of its use in early times. Each culture has utilized wood in ingenious ways. Perhaps the largest surviving collection of wood structures is to be found in Asia and the surrounding regions (figure 103). These structures have not only survived centuries of natural weathering but also the threats posed by earthquakes, fires, and insects. These consist primarily of temples and palaces and are today the cultural treasures of their respective nations. Wood has enjoyed a wide range of uses. In addition to being used as a primary structural material, it is successfully used as a wall and floor surface, as a ceiling and

Figure 102. Mosaic tile work. St. Mark's Basilica. Venice. Italy.

Figure 103. Wood buildings of Malaysia.

Figure 104. Fiber-roofed house in Africa.

Figure 105. Fiber-roofed house in England.

Figure 106. Wood-clad building. Williamsburg, Virginia.

Figure 107. Brick house in England.

Figure 108. Colorful stucco house. Trinidad, Cuba.

Figure 109. Mud-clad building. Mopti. Africa.

roofing material, and in ornamental carvings. It has the ability to receive a stain color, paint, or be left to weather naturally. Wood has a variety of graining and colors by species. It is common to all nations around the world in varying degrees and is easily cut, carved, and otherwise worked with simple tools. Of all the base materials, wood is perhaps the most versatile and diverse.

The least permanent building materials are clay and fiber. Fiber may rival wood as being the oldest material used by man in building construction. Fiber mats can be made from a variety of indigenous reeds, leaves, or fronds. While fiber is the most humble of materials, it has been used in some of the most charming and attractive ways by various cultures. The people of Africa traditionally used fibers for both wall panels and roofing material, and the resulting buildings have a sense about them that is at once true to the region and to the lifestyle of the culture (figure 104). Some older homes in England are roofed with reeds, called thatch, to achieve a unique charm and decorative affect (figure 105). The thatched roof is considered to be so aesthetically successful that some homes continue to be roofed with this material despite the availability of more durable materials.

For other cultures, the base material itself is an important contributing element of the indigenous architectural style. One such example is the use of clay, also called adobe, in the architecture of the West African countries of Mali and Togo. The people of these countries have shown great ingenuity in their use of clay and simple timbers to construct their homes and places of worship on the dry savannas. Using their indigenous materials, these people have developed architecture that adapts well to the harsh climate and the scarcity of more permanent materials (figure 109). For some cultures, the base material is a defining element of the architecture such as the wood-clad buildings of colonial America (figure 106), the red brick houses of England (figure 107), or the colorful concrete stucco of the Caribbean (figure 108). These become the material of choice because they are readily available in the locality where construction is taking place. Cultures should naturally use those materials that are easily available whether sand, clay, stone, or wood. The mid-19th-century architect Viollet-le-Duc said, "To build for the architect is to use materials according to their properties and their essential nature, with the express intention of fulfilling a purpose by the simplest and strongest means; it is furthermore to give the built structure an aspect of permanence, fitting proportions, subject to certain rules imposed by the human senses, reason, and instinct. The methods employed by the builder must therefore vary according to the nature of his materials, the financial means at his disposal, the particular requirements of each kind of building, and the culture into which he has been born."[57]

Modern Materials

The 20th century was the dawn of a new age for building construction with the introduction of steel and glass as primary building materials. These new materials challenged the role played by the noble and base materials of the past and provided new architectural opportunities of height and scale undreamed of by previous generations of architects. Architects began to experiment with steel and glass in creative ways and produced a new building form—the tall building. Buildings were no longer exclusively clad in stone or brick but put on a sleek skin of glass and steel. The traditional decorative elements of carved stone and wood, along with the metal crafter's work of iron and bronze were seldom used. In their place, architects began a century-long experiment with glass of different colors and reflection, of steel cladding, and of cast concrete. Now that we have had several generations to evaluate this experiment, we can begin to form an opinion as to its success in utilizing steel, glass, and concrete in the role of noble materials.

Architecture as Sculpture

One of the results of these new materials and building methods has been the creation of a new generation of building forms of unique shapes and materials. These new shapes have redefined what a building should, or could, look like and have produced buildings that more strongly resemble sculpture than traditional building forms. However, architecture assuming a sculptural form is not entirely a new thing. Many of the great buildings of the past made use of sculptural forms in their massing. For buildings predating the 20th century, this sculptural massing usually incorporated a dome. But beginning in the late 19th century, architects began to experiment with forms never before seen. Who can deny the impressive lines of the Eiffel Tower (1889) or the inspiring beauty of the Sydney Opera House (1957) (figures 110–111). These structures do not look back to a classical past but forward to a new era of design made possible by new materials and technology. They look nothing like the traditional concept of a building; and yet, they have captured the affection of the cities in which they are located, becoming cherished icons. They are buildings taking on the role of sculpture within the greater civic landscape.

First of all, let us define the difference between a building and a sculpture. A building differs from a sculpture in that a building is made for human use having both an exterior and an interior. This definition may help explain why, for example, the Great Pyramid is not considered to be a building, while the Taj Mahal (also a tomb) is considered to be a building. In this sense, the difference between the two being that the Great Pyramid, in its original form, did not allow access to its interior, while the Taj Mahal does have an accessible interior. Buildings are therefore usually differentiated from sculpture by their size and by the fact that they enclose an accessible and useful space. But this traditional concept began to be challenged in the 20th century when new technology and materials expanded the architect's artistic palette. Innovative building designs using the latest materials and technology began to stretch our preconceived ideas of the forms a building could achieve.

Figure 110. Eiffel Tower, Paris, France.

Figure 111. Sydney Opera House, Sydney, Australia.

What has made these new buildings unique is their complete transition from *incorporating* sculptural elements to *becoming* the sculptural element. Advances in computer automation and construction techniques have made it possible for buildings to take on fantastic shapes that just a generation ago would have been impossible to build. No longer limited by standard post and lintel designs, architects have launched into free flowing shapes that have redefined our ideas of what buildings should look like. What shall we say then about such buildings? Must buildings always have columns and capitals to be classic?

What about materials? Can we consider buildings that are clad in steel or glass to be built of noble materials? These are important questions.

One proponent of this avant-garde approach to building design is Frank Gehry. Mr. Gehry is a winner of the Pritzker Prize, the highest award for architectural achievement. He has designed many important sculptural buildings around the world.

The Guggenheim Museum in Bilbao, Spain (figure 112) is clad in titanium steel. It is amorphous in shape with its undulating surfaces. Its distinctive form has been variously described as having an allusion to boats, the organic world, and, less complimentary, as a pile of scrap metal. It has received critical acclaim and has become a popular tourist attraction for the city. While the museum exhibits modern art, it is the building itself that has become the real exhibit. This building challenges our idea of what a museum looks like.

A second building by Mr. Gehry is the Disney Center for the Performing Arts in Los Angeles (figure 113). Again, this important civic structure is clad in titanium, not limestone or granite, as a building of its type would have been a generation earlier. It is of an indefinable shape and is quite dramatic in its use of solids and voids. At night, when it is illuminated, it creates a very dramatic point of interest for the city.

Applying the principles for architectural excellence in design, we can look at these buildings with an informed eye, form an opinion as to their aesthetic success, and decide how buildings like these fit our concept of enduring architecture. These buildings represent a new type of building—architecture posing as sculpture. As a group, this is the one thing that they, and others like them, all have in common. They spring from the architect's imagination and stand alone and unique in their style and form. As unique design statements, they can become treasured assets for their cities, like the Eiffel Tower and the Sydney Opera House. Are buildings such as these examples of excellent architecture? That is the question before us.

Sculptural buildings, as such, cannot be progenitors of a widely adaptable architecture because they are not a repeatable form. They are expressions of the architect's ability as a designer and particularly as an artist. They represent imaginative solutions to particular design problems, but they in no way provide a typology for a new form of building, as did the amphitheater or basilica. Some may become beloved icons in their respective cities, but they will not be progenitors of a widely adopted new style that will be repeated in the course of commercial architecture on Main Street or the design of houses on your street. They are unique forms and therefore, are not classic in either the larger sense or the smaller sense. So, does this mean that they are inferior architecture? Not at all. However, the next big challenge facing this type of building is the unavoidable test of time. They look interesting now, but how will our eyes see them after 50 or 100 years? Will they still be admired for their bold forms, or will they be considered eyesores? How well will their novel construction and materials hold up to the weathering of the years? Time alone will tell.

Figure 112. Guggenheim Museum, Bilbao, Spain.

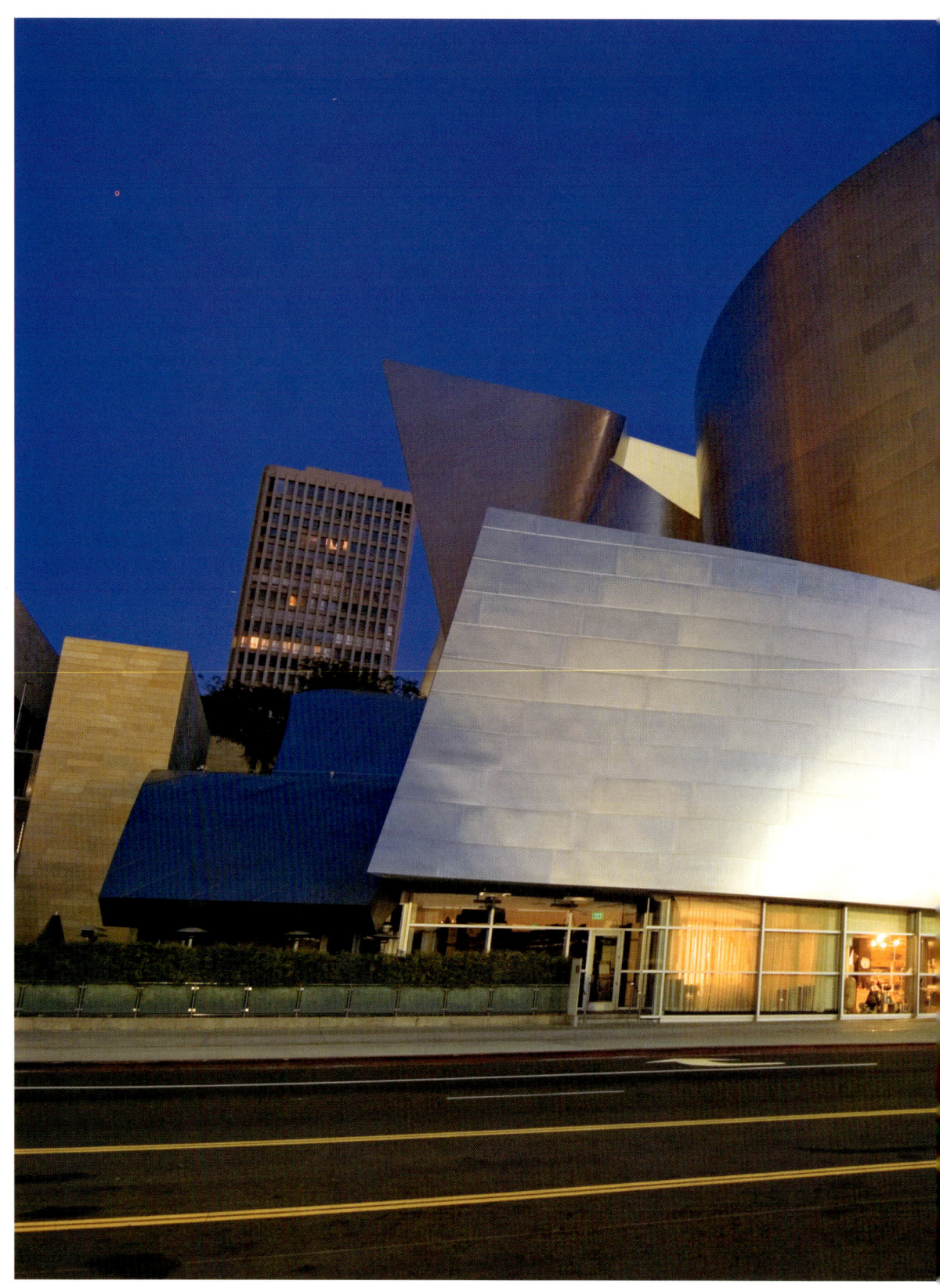
Figure 113. Disney Center for the Performing Arts, Los Angeles, California.

CHAPTER 8
TIME IS THE FINAL ARBITER

It is a challenge for any generation to evaluate the aesthetic success of its architecture because its eyes become accustomed to certain forms over time, and therefore it is difficult to adjust to new forms that vary from this norm. Otto Wagner (1841–1918) looked out upon the dawn of the 20th century and said, "The modern eye has lost a feeling for small and intimate scale, and accustomed itself to less varied images, to longer straight lines, to more extensive areas, to larger masses, which suggests we should exercise greater restraint, giving less emphasis to the outlines of such (forms)."[58] To gain a better perspective of how time is the ultimate arbiter in matters of aesthetics, let us consider a broad sample of 20th-century buildings that were considered innovative and widely admired when they were first built. Their lasting aesthetic merit can only now be made apparent, as we have looked upon them for 25 years or more, and the effect of their initial novelty is past.

Figure 114. Casa Mila, Barcelona, Spain.

Figure 115. The New York Public Library, New York City, New York.

Casa Mila, Barcelona, Spain
This landmark building by Antoni Gaudi, built in 1905–1910, reflects the organic fluidity of the Art Nouveau movement. "Petrified waves of the sea: frozen sand dunes; every sea form comes to mind when one looks at this extraordinary block of flats."[59] Like a huge sandcastle, Casa Mila's colorless stucco exterior undulates while its curving roofline mimics ocean waves. The building's fantastic chimney pots explode from the roof as solidified sea spray. The marine imagery is completed by the wrought-iron balcony railings, which appear to be mixture of seaweed and other detritus that has washed up on a beach.

The New York Public Library, New York City, New York
This Beaux-arts style building was designed by Carrère and Hastings and completed in 1911. It is clad in Indiana limestone and decorated with sculptural groups of allegorical figures representing learning and wisdom among others. The library was built to last for the ages as well as to stand as an ornament for the city. Its architecture is an expression of optimism about the future, as the First World War had not yet shattered the innocence of the age.

Figure 116. City Hall, Stockholm, Sweden.

City Hall, Stockholm, Sweden

Stockholm's City Hall, or Stadshuset, was designed by the Swedish architect Ragnar Östberg (1866–1945) and was built between 1911 and 1923 in the National Romantic style. It is an example of a country's successful attempt to create a new architecture inspired by its past that is both modern and true to its national spirit. The building is located on the island of Kungsholmen and is built around two squares, an outer courtyard and an enclosed hall. The Stadshuset's 314-foot tower features a distinctive cupola with a golden spire of three crowns, the old national symbol of Sweden. The building represents one of the few examples of a 20th-century country creating a new architectural vocabulary using the traditions and materials that are indigenous to it.

Figure 117. Villa Savoie, Poissy, France.

Villa Savoie, Poissy, France

Charles-Edouard Jeanneret (1887–1965), who assumed the name Le Corbusier, presented five principles for modern architecture. These consisted of: 1) raising the building on free-standing pillars to allow for parking underneath; 2) forming external and internal walls independent of the structural skeleton; 3) providing an open grid floor plan for maximum flexibility; 4) designing a modern façade void of ornamentation; and 5) utilizing flat roofs for outdoor living. Le Corbusier's principles are an attempt to create a new beginning point for architecture. Gideon, a contemporary of Le Corbusier, wrote of that period, "we had to begin anew as if nothing had ever been done before."[60] Le Corbusier designed a house in 1929 demonstrating these principles called the Villa Savoie in Poissy, France. Declaring that a house is a "machine for living," Le Corbusier's residential essay is severe in line and form and has few references to the more typical elements of a house. While Villa Savoie is successful as a figure of modern art, it failed in the more functional aspects required of a convenient home. The views of the lawn from the second-floor terrace are obstructed by the solid wall serving as a railing, thus defeating the visual connection to its surroundings. Furthermore, the raised floor plan precludes any physical connection to the great lawn and requires its occupants to walk full flights of steps to access the lawn from the living areas located on the second and third floors. The building's flat roof and terraces were a continual source of water problems for the owner so that the house eventually fell into disuse and disrepair over time. Today the house has been restored and is maintained by a foundation as a museum of the work of Le Corbusier.

Figure 118. Chapel of Nôtre Dame du Haut, Ronchamp, France.

Chapel of Nôtre Dame du Haut, Ronchamp, France

Ironically, Le Corbusier's famous Pilgrimage Chapel at Ronchamp built in 1955 does not make use of his five principles. In this building, Le Corbusier abandons his earlier principles and embraces the more human aspects required of a building that is to serve the needs of contemplation and worship. The chapel at Ronchamp looks nothing like his earlier experiment with the "machine for living." By relying on abstract sculptural forms, Le Corbusier was able to create a building that provided an inspiring and worshipful space. The chapel at Ronchamp proved to be widely influential on a whole generation of similar buildings and is still performing its original function today.

Figure 119. Rockefeller Center, New York City, New York.

Rockefeller Center, New York

This landmark complex of buildings was designed by Raymond Hood among others and was constructed over the years 1932–1940. It was the largest privately owned business and amusement complex in the America of its time and consists of 10 buildings on 12 acres in the heart of Manhattan. The various buildings are designed in a Corporate Modern style and are visually unified through their common use of Indiana limestone. Each building incorporates artistic works ranging from decorative bronze grills, public sculpture, carvings, embellishments and murals. The open-air sunken plaza is located in the center of the complex and was originally designed for retail tenants. The plaza initially proved to be a failure as a retail location because of its difficult visual and physical connection to pedestrian traffic on the street above. This problem was rectified when the plaza was retrofitted to serve as an ice skating rink in the winter and as an outdoor dining area during the rest of the year. The Plaza has since become one of the most successful and cherished urban sites in the city of New York.

Figure 120. The Crow Island School, Winnetka, Illinois.

The Crow Island School, Winnetka, Illinois
This school, designed by Perkins Wheeler & Will along with Eliel Saarinen and Eero Saarinen in 1939–40, represents a radical departure from traditional school design up to that time. The building's simple massing and flat façades with metal frame windows proved to be highly influential on the next generation of schools built in America. Its popularity with school boards around the country is perhaps due more to its economy of construction than any aesthetic considerations. The architecture of school buildings inspired by Crow Island appears greatly impoverished compared with the school buildings built earlier in the century.

Figure 121. The Farnsworth House, Plano, Illinois.

The Farnsworth House, Plano, Illinois

Ludwig Mies van der Rohe's weekend retreat house designed for Dr. Edith Farnsworth, is a pure expression of the tenets of the International School. It has been considered an icon of its style almost since its completion and was designated a National Historic landmark in 2006. Built between 1945 and 1951, its refined minimalist form is representative of Mies' search for an architecture that reflected the industrial technology and materials of his time and place. Designed to challenge our ideas of what a house could be, the structure consists of a white steel frame enclosing a single room with large floor-to-ceiling glass panels.

His extensive use of glass connects the occupants to the outdoors in what was then a novel and unique way. There are two free-standing service cores within the plan. One houses the kitchen, bathroom, and fireplace, while the other provides additional storage. Through the Farnsworth House, Mies was able to demonstrate, for the first time, the modernist ideals that would later define the buildings of his long career.

Figure 122. Lever House, New York City, New York.

Lever House, New York City, New York

Lever House has the distinction of being the first glass curtain-walled building in New York City. It was designed by Gordon Bunshaft/Skidmore, Owings & Merrill and was built between 1950–52. As the first of its type, its clean lines and gleaming exterior provided a striking contrast amid the street's masonry pre-war buildings. "Lever House comprises two counter posed rectangular volumes, sheathed in a thin curtain wall of stainless steel and glass, floating on a pilotis, the lower volume carrying a roof garden and enclosing a garden-atrium retreat. The mastery of proportions and especially of detailing was and remains exceptional, a harbinger of the technological excellence of the metal-glass curtain wall that was to become the special province of Late Modern builders."[61]

Figure 123. Seagram Building, New York City, New York.

Seagram Building, New York City, New York
Ludwig Mies van der Rohe designed New York's Seagram Building in 1954–58 in collaboration with Philip Johnson. The building is considered to be one of the finest examples demonstrating the ideals of the International style. Known as "glass box architecture," the building has a tinted bronze glass and steel façade and features minimal ornament in keeping with the tenets of the International School. This building has become an icon of modernism and is the original prototype for thousands of similar buildings in cities around the world. When it was new, it looked fresh and sleek in contrast to the surrounding pre-war buildings of New York. Now that 50 years have passed, and we have filled our cities with similar buildings, we can better appraise the long-term aesthetic value of such architecture and the impact it has left on the streetscapes of our cities.

FIGURE 124. VANNA VENTURI HOUSE. CHESTNUT HILL, PENNSYLVANIA.

Vanna Venturi House, Chestnut Hill, Pennsylvania

The architect Robert Venturi designed this house for his mother. It was built between 1961–64 and is an early example of an attempt to reconnect with tradition within a Modernist architectural environment. The house's architecture relies on a combination of oversized details and symbolic references to achieve its effect. These include the massive central chimney and the broken pediment of the main gable. The Venturi house's notoriety is due largely in part to its being the first of its style (early Post-Modern) in an era known for its hostility toward traditional or classic architectural references.

Figure 125. One Atlantic Center (formerly the IBM Building), Atlanta, Georgia.

One Atlantic Center (formerly the IBM Building), Atlanta, Georgia

One Atlantic Center, designed by Philip Johnson/John Burgee (1906–2005), is a successful integration of traditional design elements in the architecture of a late 20th-century office building. Johnson and Burgee clad the building in granite and glass utilizing Gothic-inspired detailing. Rather than rejecting surface ornament, Johnson embraced it and gave the building strong visual interest at street level and as seen from a distance by its bold massing. Instead of the typical flat roof, One Atlantic Center has a steeply pitched roof clad in copper and crowned by a gilded cupola. The introduction of verde green and gold in such a composition is most effective and demonstrates the architect's skill at combining noble building materials and traditional design elements in a building firmly rooted in the 20th century. Because of all these factors, One Atlantic Center has endeared itself to the city of Atlanta and is admired as one of Johnson/Burgee's most handsome commercial structures.

Figure 126. National Gallery of Art, Washington, D.C.

National Gallery of Art, Washington, D.C.
I.M. Pei's (b. 1917) East Wing Addition to the National Gallery of Art was completed in 1978 and opened to critical acclaim. The American Institute of Architects (AIA) awarded the building its 25 Year Award to commemorate the building's success. The building is clad in Tennessee Pink stone and fits a difficult triangular shaped site. This building was very influential on museum architecture for a decade, and similar museum buildings were built throughout America. This building's impact is entirely dependant on the geometry of its massing because the structure is stripped of all ornament in true Modernist form.

Figure 127. Pompidou Centre, Paris, France.

Pompidou Centre, Paris, France.
The Pompidou Centre in Paris has been the subject of debate since its construction in the early 1970s. Designed by Richard Rogers (b. 1933) and Renzo Piano (b. 1937), the building has been called "Europe's most daring cultural building of the 20th century." The building's exterior is characterized by an exoskeleton of steel, stylized technological adornment, and by exterior escalator tubes that diagonally cross the façade. Furthermore, the building's mechanical systems are exposed on the surface of the building with each system painted a different primary color. The exterior glass walls make the interior feel as open as possible and further expose the interior steel structure to view from the street. The core of the building is essentially an open plan and includes an exhibition area, an art museum, and a movie theater. The building's strong industrial aesthetic has caused it to be called a "refinery" by its detractors. Located in a historic residential district of Paris, it stands in marked contrast to the surrounding buildings, neither relating to what came before nor adding grace to its immediate environment.

We learn from this survey of landmark buildings that variety and diversity is the norm. While some of these buildings have proven to be more enduring than others, each announced a new direction in the architecture of its day. Some influenced an entire generation of buildings while others had a more marginal effect. Each is a reflection of its particular time and place; each speaks of the values and priorities of the society that built it; and each incorporates the five principles to varying degrees. Therefore, it is worthwhile studying and contemplating them in order to judge to what extent each building is sympathetic to the five principles. Then we can gain a better understanding of the impact these principles have on a building's lasting success. As we build for the future, let us more fully appreciate the influence of these principles on our architecture's excellence.

CHAPTER 9
THE NEW MILLENNIUM

Standing at the dawn of the new millennium, we have the advantage of being able to look back over thousands of years upon the architecture of our shared past. We can reflect on the development and use of a wide divergence of materials. We have building and service technologies unthinkable in previous centuries. We can see the end effect of mature architectural styles ranging from the classicism of Greece to the 20th century's functionalist geometric forms. It is self-evident that the course for architectural excellence is not made up of a single stylistic dogma, but rather is composed of a variety of individual movements which are all expressions of the same art form. Each of these, in its turn, has worked toward the advancement of man's goal of creating enclosure of space in some new and effective way. Like scientific discoveries, these architectural movements have contributed new source material in man's quest to solve this common problem. Each is worthy of further study to discover the subtleties and nuances of their novel approach. As we build the architectural fabric for our time, we must choose between the well-trodden path of a culturally neutral architecture or a more demanding path that leads to architecture of cultural diversity and variety. This new architecture of excellence embracing diversity and variety will speak from the shared experience of a common past while striving to create a rich environment of enduring character. It will embody elements of style appropriate for each people as it expresses their unique personality.

The Challenge as Voiced by Others
"Make no little plans; they have no magic to stir men's blood. Make big plans; aim high in hope and work, remembering that a noble diagram once recorded will never die."[62]
  Daniel H. Burnham (1846–1912)

"Architecture is neither a fashion nor something eternal but is part of an epoch; not everything, but the essence of an epoch, an expression of its energy ... this essence is the evolving form that is not invented, but which we are working on without being aware of it. And when this great form is fully understood, then the epoch is over-then there is something new."[63]
  Ludwig Mies van der Rohe (1886–1969)

"We are looking for the reflection in architecture of the progress our own period has made towards consciousness of itself—of its special limitations and potentialities, needs, and aims. Architecture can give us insight into this process just because it is so bound up with the life of a period as a whole. Everything in it, from its fondness for certain shapes to the approaches to specific building problems which it finds most natural, reflects the condition of the age from which it springs. It is the product of all sorts of factors—social, economic, scientific, technical, and ethnological."[64]
  Sigfried Gideon (1888–1968)

"Most contemporary movements have failed to achieve a dialogue with the past: modernists rejected the past, postmodernists merely borrowed elements from the past in post-modern pastiche, neo-classicists try simply to imitate the past, and deconstructivists have done little more than combine strategies of the modernists and the postmodernists."[65]
  Thomas Leddy (b. 1949)

"The art of building faithfully portrays the social history of the people whose needs it ministers. We must remember, therefore, that principles of action, perception, convictions, habits of thought, and customs are the directors of all architectural design."[66]
  Calvert Vaux (1824–1895)

"Each country has been given its own characteristics by its Creator and should work out its own salvation. The best architecture of the past has always been native to its own country and has grown out of a thorough knowledge of the local requirements and conditions. Requirements include body, mind, and spirit. Conditions include Climate and National Character."[67]

Charles F. Annesley Voysey (1857–1941)

"What is architecture anyway? Is it the vast collection of various buildings which have been built to please the varying taste of the various lords of mankind? I think not. No, I know that architecture is life; or at least it is life itself taking form and therefore it is the truest record of life as it was lived in the world yesterday, as it is lived today or ever will be lived. So architecture I know to be a Great Spirit. Architecture is that great living spirit which from generation to generation, from age to age, proceeds, persists, creates, according to the nature of man, and his circumstances as they change. That is really architecture."[68]

Frank Lloyd Wright (1867–1959)

"Man is by nature a creator. After the likeness of his Maker, man is born to create: to fashion beauty, to originate new values. That is his supreme vocation. This truth awakens a resonant response deep within us, for we know that one of the most intense joys that the soul of man can experience is that of creative activity."[69]

H.E. Huntley

The Challenge of Expediency
Expediency is one of the biggest challenges to achieving great architecture for both the architect and the client. Architects sometimes adopt that which is tried and true because it is the quickest and most economical approach. With computer aided drafting, this threat is even more real as firms develop extensive electronic libraries of building sections and details. The temptation to repeatedly reuse these details is great because of the cost savings and time efficiency that such files provide. Furthermore, the demand from clients for rapid production of drawings combined with the large volume of work that inevitably comes to the most talented firm results in pressure to limit the amount of time allowed for reflection and creativity. The best architects successfully achieve the balance needed for thoughtful evaluation of client needs, site restrictions, budget constraints, and artistic creativity.

As architect Craig Ellwood puts it, "Impatience is part of the problem, as too many of us are caught up in the race to be first in creating a new architecture. There seems to exist among our leading architects a mass denial for continuity. Each new project is treated as a separate essay in abstract design, without any affiliation to what the past has taught us, without any real concern for the present, without any relationship to the work of other architects."[70]

Managing expediency in commercial work is a frequent challenge because commercial developers expect construction documents to be produced quickly and the building to be designed with the goal of keeping construction costs to a minimum. Commercial structures are especially at risk because of the profit oriented nature of business. Yet, it is a tragedy for a city's built environment to be filled with such uninspired structures. Too many of the world's cities are a monotonous forest of concrete and glass towers of little distinction. The ideal for any building is to make a tangible contribution to the fabric of the city in both its design and its function. Therefore, the challenge for clients is to provide their architects with the time and budgets required to achieve greatness or at least dignity in their work. The challenge for architects is to develop a natural sensitivity to these principles so that even common buildings can be transformed into aesthetically contributing structures within normal budgets.

The Challenge for Educational Training
The identification of students with promise and the training of them is the most critical component in a nation's effort to achieve a high level of architectural design. All other contributing factors can be in place, but if the

talent is not developed, then these efforts will be in vain. The foundation for a future architectural career is a first-class education that includes a firm knowledge of the sciences, mathematics, language, history, geography, music, and the arts. Such an education is necessary in order to give the budding architect the knowledge base from which creative talents can develop. Even Vitruvius in the 1st century B.C. considered a broad educational background to be critical for the future success of an architect.[71] This training can begin as early as the primary school level so that students can be nurtured to develop their visual and spatial skills. Plato quotes Socrates as having said, "The man who would apply himself to this goal (aesthetic appreciation) must begin, when he is young, by applying himself to the contemplation of physical beauty."[72] Therefore, students must be taught to see using the best examples of architecture and art. Studies by the psychologist Eysenck have found that creativity as an achievement has its basis in a broad educational background and is, of course, dependent on the opportunity to put that creativity into practice. Failing to give students the chance to acquire this foundational knowledge may cause them to miss their life's calling as far as genuine, socially valued and creative activity is concerned.[73] As these students progress in their studies, they can be taught the fundamentals of proportion and scale in basic geometry courses. Drawing skills can be developed and honed. Those students demonstrating a natural talent for architecture can be directed to professional programs. Other students who do not appear to have the right skill set, but who have a love for architecture, can be directed to one of the allied arts or trades.

Societies have historically taken a passive approach to identifying architectural talent. Yet many of these same societies place great emphasis on identifying athletic, musical, and academic talent and nurturing these through vigorous training programs beginning at an early age. Think of the benefit to a society if it made a concerted effort to identify students and nurture them for the craft of architecture or one of its related trades. Imagine the number of persons of real talent lost to society because no such program exists. Architecture programs allied with the building sciences can offer students having an interest in architecture, but lacking the required aptitude, the opportunity to direct their talents into one of these other areas. In this way, the total team of professionals required for great architecture can be developed.

The challenge for academia in such a program is to strike the right balance between being too dogmatic on one extreme or totally void of any real theory on the other. Consequently, when academia fails to establish meaningful principles to guide their students' aesthetic development, the result is architecture of little lasting value for the culture. To avoid such a failure, architecture schools need to adopt principles for architectural excellence that will provide a foundation for future work. When fully trained in these principles, architects and design professionals can lead their culture on the path to excellence. To forego the training of design professionals in the principles of aesthetics is to condemn a culture to a built environment of uninspired architecture.

The Challenge of Government Patronage
The greatest opportunities for architectural greatness lie in those societies experiencing population and economic growth. When this is the case, governments must make use of the opportunity to manage that growth intelligently by long-term city planning, by constructing municipal infrastructure designed to last centuries, by creating neighborhood zoning restrictions and by enacting building codes to ensure quality of construction. A municipal building department is required to enforce these fundamental components. In some societies, this role occasionally resides in a single individual such as the head of government. In others, this responsibility resides in an inspired official having an educated staff to support the effort to achieve civic greatness. Furthermore, governments must encourage the development of professional architectural practices within their country. Relying on architectural services from foreign nations frequently results in an architecture that does not reflect the local culture.

Because heads of government and governmental agencies are the primary patrons for civic works of architecture, they set the tone for their nation's level of taste. It is a role of great responsibility because the resulting architecture is to stand for centuries. Beyond the obvious importance of city halls, capitols, court houses and the like, the same careful consideration should be given to the more common and numerous buildings of everyday life such as government offices, schools, libraries, or recreation centers. Government leaders who ignore the matter of good taste in this tangible area under their direct control fail their society and fail to demonstrate the leadership required of them. Government leaders should thoughtfully seek to maintain high standards for their works of architecture and art as they strive to attain a point of cultural classicism. Numerous architects and artists from the past achieved aesthetic success in their public buildings. These buildings have stood the test of time and are a cherished legacy for their respective cities and nations. Governments who maintain this high standard will be rewarded with an architecture that serves its purpose and ennobles the built environment of their communities for centuries to come.

A Call for Excellence in Architecture
True excellence in architecture is characterized by a living architecture that is not threatened by references to past traditions but finds inspiration in them. True excellence in architecture is able to be understood rationally and thus be emulated by designers and architects of various skills and talent. It appreciates the natural proportions and rhythms found in Nature. It does not avoid the use of ornament and uses it to articulate the building's surface to provide visual delight. It meets the functional requirements of today's business world and the needs of contemporary family life. The architects of the new millennium must take the lead in creating architecture of excellence for their respective societies. This architecture will make use of the best materials, the most recent technology, and meet the societal demands of each culture. This architecture will embrace, not reject, the principles of aesthetics and will enhance the dignity of the built environment. It will be architecture of such breadth that it will be relevant for use on a house, a church, a town hall, a school, a commercial building, or a museum. The great architecture of our past displayed this sort of breadth, and the best architecture of the future will do so as well.

Author's Acknowledgements

This book has been a work of love for me these past four years. It is a work of love that expresses my passion for architecture and a work of love for those architects and designers who are to come after me. The effort and time expended was significant and therefore, I wish to thank, first of all, my family for their generous support and encouragement.

I am grateful to my publishers, Paul Latham and Alessina Brooks, for believing in the importance of this project, and to my editor, Beth Browne, Joe Boschetti and Rod Gilbert of Images Publishing, Australia, for their support in publishing this book. I also wish to offer a special thanks to Kent Hatterick and Amanda Byrom at Beck Premedia Workflow Compression, Atlanta, Georgia for their assistance in typesetting the book. Amanda was most patient to allow me to literally sit beside her as she carefully assembled the images and placed them within the text.

Lastly, I wish to thank the many photographers, whose keen eye and skill in their craft so wonderfully captured the essence of some of the world's greatest architecture. Because architecture is a form of visual art, photography is a critical means of communicating its subtleties to those not able to experience the buildings and their interiors in person. As such, it preserves for all time—sometimes outliving the very structures themselves—a reflection of the works of man's hand for ages to come.

Picture Acknowledgements

I am most grateful to the institutions and individuals who have contributed graphic material for use in this book. In all cases, diligent effort has been made to contact the copyright holders. However, if there are any errors or omissions, the publisher and I would be pleased to correct or insert the appropriate credits in any subsequent edition of this book.

Abbeville Press, Figure 36.
Alex Bartel/Esto, Figure 111.
Arcaid, Figures 46, 47.
Art Resource, Inc., Figures 7, 8, 17, 18, 22, 34, 37, 41, 42, 79, 81, 122, 123.
Artifice, Figures 2, 39, 113, 120.
Artists Rights Society (ARS), Figures 117, 118.
Bill Maris/Esto, Figure 124.
Casey Sills Photography, Figures 53, 54, 55.
Craig S. Kaplan, Figure 62.
Dreamstime.com, pp. i, ii, iv-v, viii-ix, xi, xii, xv, xvi, Figures 1, 3, 6, 9, 10, 12, 13, 21, 23, 25, 26, 27, 29, 30, 31, 32, 35, 38, 45, 64, 65, 66, 75, 77, 78, 85, 87, 88, 89, 90, 92, 93, 95, 97, 99, 100, 102, 103, 104, 105, 106, 107, 109, 110, 114, 127, 128.
Ezra Stoller/Esto, Figure 126.
Fritz von Schulenburg Photography, Figures 43, 44.
Intbau, Figure 56.
Istockphoto.com, Figures 11, 17, 24, 28, 40, 76, 91, 96, 108, 116, 121, 125.
Kohn, Pedersen, Fox Associates, Figure 98.
Merrill, Pastor, and Colgan Architects, Figures 52, 55.
Peter Aaron/Esto, Figures 115, 119.
Ralph Richter/archenova/Esto, Figure 112.
Robert A. M. Stern Architects, Figure 101.
Thomas Mayer, Thomasmayerarchive.com, Figure 113.

Figure 128. Byodo-in temple, Uji, Japan.

NOTES

1. Philip Johnson expressed a similar sentiment in his 1979 acceptance speech for the Pritzker Prize.

2. H.E. Huntley, *The Divine Proportion* (New York: Dover Publications, 1970), 20.

3. Adolf Loos, "Ornament und Verbrechen" (1908), in id., *Trotzdem 1900–1930* (Innsbruck: 1931).

4. Paul Heyer, *Architects on Architecture* (New York: Walker and Company, 1966), 22.

5. Ralph Weber, "The Myth of Meaningful Forms," *Philosophy and Architecture* (Amsterdam, 1994): 117.

6. Leone Battista Alberti, *The Ten Books of Architecture*, bk 1, chapter 9, trans. James Leoni (New York: Dover Publications, 1986), 13.

7. Paul Heyer, *Architects on Architecture*, 51.

8. Eugene-Emmanuel Viollet-le-Duc, *Lectures on Architecture*, vols. 1 and 2, trans. Benjamin Bucknall (New York: Dover Publications, 1987).

9. W.E. Begley, *Taj Mahal: The Illumined Tomb* (Cambridge: Harvard Univ. and MIT Press, 1989), xliv.

10. Ibid., xli.

11. Morris Bishop, *A Survey of French Literature* (New York: Harcourt, Brace, and World, 1955), 114.

12. H.J. Eysenck, *Sense and Nonsense in Psychology* (London: Pelican Press, 1957), quoted in H.E. Huntley, *The Divine Proportion* (New York: Dover Publications, 1970), 319.

13. Frank Lloyd Wright, *The Japanese Print: An Interpretation* (New York: Horizon, 1967).

14. Frank Lloyd Wright, "In the Cause of Architecture," *Architectural Record* 23 (1908): 155–221. Repr. New York: 1975, ed. Frederick Gutheim. A summary of these points is found in Hanno-Walter Kruft, *A History of Architectural Theory* (New York: Princeton Arch. Press, 1994), 425.

15. "Big House on the Prairie," *Period Homes*, May 2005, 13–15.

16. Frank Lloyd Wright, *The Future of Architecture* (New York: Horizon, 1953), 321–22.

17. Frank Lloyd Wright, *The Natural House* (New York: Horizon, 1954), 44.

18. Heyer, *Architects on Architecture*, 103.

19. Heyer, *Architects on Architecture*, (includes an interview with Harry Weese), 43.

20. Huntley, *The Divine Proportion*, 80.

21. Percy Gardner, *The Principles of Greek Art* (New York and London: Macmillan, 1921), 319–320.

22. Herbert Koch, *Von Nochleben des Vitru* (Baden-Baden: 1951), 9.

23. Leone Battista Alberti, *The Ten Books of Architecture*, bk 1, chapter 9, 14.

24. Andrea Palladio, *I quattro libri dell'architettura 1570* (Repr. in New York: Dover Publications, 1965), 6.

25. Andrea Palladio, *I quattro libri dell'architettura 1570* (Repr. in New York: Dover Publications, 1986), 38.

26. *Encyclopedie, ou Dictionnaire raisonne des sciences, des arts et des meitiers* (1751 onwards); the first volume of plates, in which architecture has an important place, did not appear until 1761.

27. W.A. Eden, "St. Thomas Aquinas and Vitruvius," *Mediaeval and Renaissance Studies* 2, (Warburg Institute, 1950): 183–85.

28. Heyer, *Architects on Architecture*, (includes an interview with Mies van der Rohe), 36.

29. Roland Fréart de Chambrey, *Parallele d'l architecture antique et de la moderne*, (Paris 1650; 1702); trans. John Evelyn (London: 1664); facs. repr. of the latter (1970), 7.

30. Geoffrey Scott, *Architecture of Humanism: A Study in the History of Taste* (New York: 1914, 1924; repr. New York/London: W.W. Norton, 1999), 150.

31. Vitruvius, *The Ten Books on Architecture*, trans. Morris Hicky Morgan (Harvard Univ. Press, 1914; New York: Dover Publications, 1960), 13. Citations are to the Dover edition.

32. Ibid., 103.

33. Ibid., 104–106.

34. Ibid., 17.

35. Begley, *Taj Mahal: The Illumined Tomb*, xliii.

36. Alphonse Mucha, *Lectures on Art* (New York: St. Martin's Press, 1975), 11.

37. Arthur Comey, "Maximum Building Height Regulation," *Landscape Architecture* 3 (October 1912): 19–24.

38. Alberti, *The Ten Books of Architecture*, bk 1, chapter 9, 13.

39. Vitruvius, *The Ten Books on Architecture*, 72.

40. Giuseppe Terragni, "Per un'architettura italiana moderna," *La Tribuna* 23 (March 1931) in *Cinnamon* (1976): 242ff.

41. Augustin-Charles d'Avilier, *Dictionnaire d'Architecture ou explication de tous les termes* (Paris: 1693), 229.

42. Alberti, *The Ten Books of Architecture*, bk 9, chapter 7, 201.

43. Joel Primack and Nancy Abrams, *The View from the Center of the Universe*, (New York: Riverhead Books, 2006), 156–178.

44. Ibid., 203.

45. Mucha, *Lectures on Art*, 12–13.

46. Heyer, *Architects on Architecture*, 392.

47. Louis Sullivan, "The Tall Office Building Artistically Considered," in id., *Louis Sullivan: The Public Papers* (Chicago and London: Univ. of Chicago Press, 1988), 113. First published in *Lippincott's Magazine* 57 (March 1896): 409.

48. John Wellborn Root, "The Value of Type in Art." In: ed. Donald Hoffman, *The Meanings of Architecture: Buildings and Writings by John Wellborn Root* (New York: Horizon, 1967), 169–71. First published in: *Inland Architect and Builder* 2, (November 1883): 132.

49. Heyer, *Architects on Architecture*, 207.

50. Louis-Ambroise Dubut, *Architecture Civile. Maison de ville et de campagne de toutes formes et de tous genres*, (Paris: J.M. Eberhart, 1803; 1837; Unterschneid-heim: facs. repr. of 1803 ed., 1974), Introduction.

51. Heyer, *Architects on Architecture*, (includes an interview with Louis Kahn), 392.

52. Sigfried Gideon, *Space, Time and Architecture*, (Cambridge: Harvard Univ. Press, 1967), 388–389.

53. Dankmar Adler, "The Influence of Steel Construction and Plate Glass Upon Style," in: *The Proceedings of the Thirteenth Annual Convention of the American Institute of Architects*, (1896) 58–64; repr., ed. Lewis Mumford, *Roots of Contemporary American Architecture* (New York: Grove Press, 1972), 244f.

54. The Chicago Tribune, The International Competition for a *New Administration Building for the Chicago Tribune MCMXXII*, (Chicago: 1923; facs. repr. New York: 1980), 31.

55. Kruft, *A History of Architectural Theory*, 430.

56. Allen Carlson, *Existence, Location, and Function, Philosophy and Architecture*, ed. Michael Mitias (Amsterdam and Atlanta: Rodopi Press, 1994), 153.

57. Eugene Emmanuel Viollet-le-Duc, *Dictionnaire raisonne' de l'architecture francaise du XI au XVI siecle*, (Paris: 1854–68; facs. repr. Paris: 1967) vol. 4 (1859), 1.

58. Otto Wagner, "Moderne Architektur," *Seinen Schulern ein Fuhrer auf die-sem Kunstgebiete*, (Vienna: 1895; 1899; 1902). Fourth edition entitled *Die Baukunst unserer Zeit. Dem Baukunstjünger ein Führer auf diesem Kunstgebiete* (Vienna: 1914; repr. 1979).

59. Geoffrey Warren, *Art Nouveau* (London: Octopus Books Ltd., 1972), 21.

60. Sigfried Gideon, *Architecture, You and Me* (Cambridge: Harvard Univ. Press, 1958), 26.

61. Marvin Trachtenberg and Isabelle Hyman, *Architecture from Prehistory to Post-Modernism*, (New York: Prentice Hall, 2002), 545.

62. Daniel Burnham, quoted in Kruft, *A History of Architectural Theory*, 362.

63. Heyer, *Architects on Architecture*, 27–28.

64. Gideon, *Space, Time and Architecture*, 19.

65. Thomas Leddy, *Dialogical Architecture, Philosophy and Architecture*, ed. Michael Mitias, (Amsterdam/Atlanta: Rodopi, 1994), 197.

66. Calvert Vaux, *Villas and Cottages, A Series of Designs Prepared for Execution in the United States*, (1864; repr. New York: Dover Publications, 1970), 32f.

67. Charles F. Annesley Voysey, "Patriotism in Architecture," *Architectural Association Journal* 28 (1912): 21–25.

68. Frank Lloyd Wright, quoted in ed. Bruce Brooks Pfeiffer and Gerald Nordland, *Frank Lloyd Wright: In the Realm of Ideas*, (Carbondale and Edwardsville: Southern Illinois University, 1998), 15.

69. Huntley, *The Divine Proportion*, 20.

70. Heyer, *Architects on Architecture*, 151.

71. Vitruvius, *The Ten Books on Architecture*, 5ff.

72. Plato, *Symposium*, quoted in Huntley, *The Divine Proportion*, 12–13.

73. H.J. Eysenck, *Genius* (Cambridge: Cambridge University Press, 1995), 286.

INDEX

References in bold indicate photographs and diagrams.

15 Central Park West, New York City	89, **89**
333 Wacker Drive, Chicago	86–87, **86**
Abbey Library of St. Gallen, Switzerland	36
Abrams, Nancy	73
Acropolis, Athens	6–7
Adelcrantz, Carl Fredrik	44
Adler, Dankmar	82
Aegean art	61
African architecture	94
American Institute of Architects	114
Akbar, Jalaluddin Muhammad	11
Alberti, Leone Battista	4, 36, 71
Alhambra, Granada	62–65, **64, 65**
Alys Beach, Florida	53, **57**
Amber Fort, Jaipur	**xiii**
American architecture	17–21, 53–54, 95
American Indian culture	19, 21
Amphitheatres	77, **77**
Aquinas, Thomas	50
Arabic numbering system	68
Art Deco style	84
Art Nouveau	103
Arts and Crafts Exhibition Society	47
Arts and Crafts Movement	46–49
Athena	26
Athens, Greece	26, 53
Barbaro, Daniele	36
Basilica, Vicenza	37, **37**
Bauhaus	4, 86
Beaux-arts style	103
Begley, W.E.	12, 62
Beijing, China	31–34
Berlage, Hendrik Petrus	3
Bernini, Gian Lorenzo	16
Blondel, Jacques-François	41
Borozzi, Jacopo	*see* Vignola
Burgee, John	87, 113
Burlington, Lord	38
Burnham, Daniel H.	116
Byodo-in Temple, Uji	**121**
Byzantine architecture	36, 79
Caesarea, Israel	77
Callicrates	26, 27
Callimachus	53
Carrere, John Mervin	103
Carson, Pirie, Scott Building, Chicago	82, **82**
Caryae	6
Casa Mila, Barcelona	**102**, 103
Central American architecture	3
Central Park, New York City	89
Cesar Pelli & Associates	87
Chapel of Nôtre Dame du Haut, Ronchamp	106, **106**
Charles-Edouard Jeanneret-Gris	*see* Le Corbusier
Chartres Cathedral, France	79–80, **80**
Château de Chenonceau, France	**81**
Chicago Tribune Building, Chicago	84, **84**
Chicago, Illinois	19, 82
Chichen Itza, Yucatan	**3**
Chinese architecture	14, 30–34, **31**, **32–33**, **34**, 35
Chiswick House, England	38, **39**
Christian architecture	78–80
Christianity	78
Chrysler Building, New York City	84, 85
Chrysler	84
Church of the Holy Apostles, Turkey	79
City Hall, Stockholm	104, **104**
Classical orders	14, **15**, **50**, 51, **52**, 53, 58, 72
Classicism	14
Comey, Arthur	67
Composite order	14, **15**, 58
Constantine I	78
Constantinople, Turkey	79, 90
Corinthian order	14, **15**, 30, 51, **52** 58, 72
Corporate Modern style	107
Crow Island School, Winnetka	108, **108**
Gustav, Crown Prince of Sweden	44–45
D'Aviler, Charles Augustin	71
da Vinci, Leonardo	16
de Chambray, Roland Fréart	50
Delos, Greece	77
Delphi, Greece	77
Diderot	41
Dionysus	77
Disney Center for the Performing Arts, Los Angeles	98, **100–101**
Doric column	14, **15**, **50**, 51, 58
Edward VII	16
Edwardian style	16
Egyptian architecture	3, 14, 60, 61, 90, 91
Egyptian art	60–61
Eiffel Tower, Paris	95, **96**, 98
Elizabeth I	16
Elizabethan style	16
Ellwood, Craig	117
English architecture	16, 46–49, 53, 94
Enlightenment	41
Eysenck, H.J.	16–17, 118
Fallingwater, Pennsylvania	19–21, **20**
Farnsworth House, Plano, Illinois	109, **109**
Farnsworth, Dr. Edith	109
Fibonacci sequence	69–71, **69**, 71
Fibonacci, Leonardo	68
Forbidden City, Beijing	31–34, **31**, **32–33**, **34**, 35
French architecture	16, 41, 44, 45, 72
French neo-classicism	41, 44, 72
Gabriel, Ange-Jacques	72
Gardner, Percy	26
Gaudi, Antoni	103
Gehry, Frank	97–98
George I	16
George II	16
George III	16
George IV	16

126

Georgian style	16	Latin numbering system	68
German architecture	45	Le Corbusier	82, 84, 105, 106
Gideon, Sigfried	82, 105, 116	Leddy, Thomas	116
Gilbert, Cass	82, 84	Lescot, Pierre	5–7
Goldberg, Bertrand	4	Loos, Adolph	3
Golden Mean	**67**, 68, 69, 71, 73, **74**	Louis XIV	16, 41
Golden rectangle	67, **67**, 68, **68**	Louis XV	16, 72
Gothic style	41, 46, 47, 49, 68, 79, 82–84, 113	Louis XVI	16
Goujon, Jean	6	Louvre, Paris	5–7, **8–9**
Great Pyramid, Giza	95	Lu, Peter	61
Great Pyramid, Chichen Itza	**3**	Luytens, Edward	49
Greek architecture	3, 6, 14, 22–27, 36, 41, 49, 50–51, 68, 77, 90	Mahal, Mumtaz	10
Greek mythology	26, 77	Mali, Africa	94
Gropius, Walter	84	Martin, Jean	6
Guggenheim Museum, Bilbao	97–98, **99**	Mayan architecture	3
Gustavian style	45	McAllister, Charles Warren	22
Hadith	62	Mesopotamian architecture	**2**, 3, 91
Hadrian	30	Middle Ages	37, 79
Haga Pavilion, Stockholm, Sweden	**45**	Middle Eastern architecture	62
Hagia Sophia, Istanbul	xiv, **xv**, 79	Mies van der Rohe, Ludwig	84, 86, 109, 111, 116
Hastings, Thomas	103	Minoan art	61
Helios	26	Modernist architecture	4, 112, 114
Henry II	5	Mohammed V	62
Hitchcock, Henry-Russell	84	Monticello, Virginia	38, **39**
Hood, Raymond M.	84, 107	Morgan, Morris	51
Hôtel de Soubise, Paris	**40**	Morris, William H.	47
House of Venus, Pompeii	**81**	Mosque of Mohammed Ali, Cairo	70
Houses of Parliament, London	47, **46–47**	Mucha, Alphonse	74
Howells, John Mead	84	Mughal architecture	10–12
Humayun, Nasiruddin Mohammed	11	Museum of Modern Art, New York City	84
Huntley, H.E.	117	National Gallery of Art, Washington, DC	114, **114**
Ictinus	26, 27	National Romantic style	104
Indian architecture	10–11, 14, 62	Nature	xv, 1, 2, 5, 14, 18, 21, 30, 37, 51, 66, 68, 69, 71, 119
International style	19, 84–87, 109, 111	Neo-Classicism	41
Ionic order	14, **15**, **50**, 51, 58, 68	Neo-Gothic architecture	82–84
Ishtar Gate	**2**	Neutra, Richard	84
Islamic architecture	10–12, 61–65	New Albany, Ohio	53
Islamic art	61–65	New York City, New York	84, 89, 107, 111
Islamic star patterns	61–62, **62**	New York Public Library, New York	103, **103**
Italianate style	49	Nike	26
Jahan, Shah	10, 12	Oia, Santorini	**iv–v**
Jahangir, Nuruddin Salim	11	One Atlantic Center, Atlanta	113, **113**
Japanese art	17, 21	Ornament	xv, xii, 2, 3–5, 119
Jefferson, Thomas	38	Östberg, Ragna	104
Johnson, Philip	84, 87, 111, 113	Pagan architecture	78
Johnson/Burgee Architects	87	Palazzo Vecchio, Florence	**81**
Jones, Inigo	38	Palladio, Andrea	36–38, **36**, 41, 51
Kahn, Louis I.	76	Pantheon, Rome	xiv, 27–30, **28–29**, **30**, 90
Kant	66	Parthenon, Athens	xiv, 23, **24–25**, 26–27, 90
Kaplan, Craig S.	62	Parthenon, Nashville	**26**
Kauffman, Edgar	19	Peachtree Tower, Atlanta	87, **87**
Kendall/Heaton Architects	87	Pei, I.M.	114
Koch, Herbert	36	Perkins Wheeler and Will	108
Kohn Pedersen Fox Associates PC	86	Petit Trianon, Versailles	72, **72–73**
Koran	12, 62	Petronas Towers, Kuala Lumpur, Malaysia	87–89, **87**
Kremlin cathedral, Moscow, Russia	70	Phidias	26
Kungsholmen, Sweden	104	Philae Temple, Aswan	**ii**
La Rotunda, Vicenza	38, **38**	Piano, Renzo	115
Laconia, Greece	6	Place de la Concorde, Paris	**42–43**
Lahori, Ustad Ahmad	10	Planck length	73
Lama Temple, Beijing, China	**x–xi**	Plato	118
Landshut, Bavaria	**10**	Pollio, Marcus Vitruvius	*see* Vitruvius

Polycleitus the Younger	77
Pompeii, Italy	81
Pompidou Centre, Paris	115, **115**
Porch of the Caryatides, Athens	6, **6**
Poseidon	26
Post-Modern architecture	86–87, 112
Poundbury, England	53, **57**
Prarie School	17–21
Primack, Joel	73
Pritzker Prize	97
Protestant Reformation, 1500s	80
Pugin, Augustus Welby Northmore	46
Pythagoras	68
Queen's House, England	38, **39**
Regence style	16
Regency style	16
Rehn, Jean Eric	44
Renaissance architecture	34–37, 71, 73, 77, 81
Richardson, H.H.	80
Robie House, Chicago	**18**, 19
Robins, Gay	60
Rockefeller Center, New York City	107, **107**
Rococo	41
Rogers, Richard	115
Roman classicism	37
Romanesque architecture	36
Roman architecture	3, 14, 27–30, **28–29**, **30**, 34, 36, 41, 49, 77, 79, 81, 91
Rosemary Beach, Florida	53, **55**
Royal Palace, Stockholm	44–45, **44**
Rusconi, Giovannantonio	**23**
Saarinen, Eero	108
Saarinen, Eliel	84, 108
Salle des Caryatides, Paris	6–7, **7**
Santa Maria Maggiore, Rome	**78**, 79
Scamozzi, Vincenzo	36, 41
Schrödinger, Erwin	50
Scott, Geoffrey	51
Sculpture	2, 95–98
Seagram Building, New York City	86, 111, **111**
Seaside, Florida	53, **54**
Selene	26
Serlio, Sebastiano	51
SLCE Architects	89
Socrates	118
Sparta, Greece	77
St. Mark's Basilica, Venice	79, **79**, 90, **91**
Steinhardt, Peter	61
Stern, Robert A.M	89
Sullivan, Louis	17, 76, 82, 86
Swedish architecture	44–45, 104
Swedish neo-classicism	44–45
Sweeney, Karen A.	19
Sydney Opera House	95, **97**, 98
Taj Mahal, Agra, India	10–12, **10–11**, **12**, **13**, 62, **63**, 95
Temple at Karnak, Thebes	**xvi**
Temple of Pura Ulun, Danu Bratan	**viii–ix**
Terragni, Giuseppe	68
Theater of Aspendus, Turkey	77, **77**
Theater of Epidauros, Greece	77
Tidewater, Virginia	71
Togo, Africa	94
Tomb of Humayun, Nizamuddin	11, **11**
Tradition	xii, 22–49
Treasury, Petra	**70**
Trinity Church, Boston	80, **80**
Tudor style	16
Tuscan order	14, **15**, 58
van Alen, William	84
Vanna Venturi House, Chestnut Hill	112, **112**
Vaux, Calvert	116
Venturi, Robert	112
Versailles, France	72
Vicenza, Italy	37
Victoria, Queen	16
Victorian style	16
Vignola	41, 51, 54, 58
Villa Malcontenta, Italy	38, **38**
Villa Savoie, Poissy	105, **105**
Viollet-le-Duc, Eugene-Emmanuel	5, 95
Vitruvius	xii, 6, 36, 38, 51, 53, 73, 118
Voltaire	41
Voysey, Charles F. Annesley	49, 117
Wagner, Otto	102
Watercolor, Florida	53
Weber, Ralph	3
Weese, Harry	22
Windsor, Florida	53, **56**
Woolworth Building, New York City	82–84, **83**
"Woolworth Gothic" style	84
Wright, Frank Lloyd	17–19, **17**, 84, 117
Wyatville, Sir Jeffry	46
Yusuf I	62

Every effort has been made to trace the original source of copyright material contained in this book. The publishers would be pleased to hear from copyright holders to rectify any errors or omissions.

The information and illustrations in this publication have been prepared and supplied by the author. While all reasonable efforts have been made to source the required information and ensure accuracy, the publishers do not, under any circumstances, accept responsibility for errors, omissions and representations express or implied.